Sherlock Holmes
and the
Hilldrop Crescent
Mystery

Val Andrews

with an introduction by
David James Smith

First published in 2011 by
The Irregular Special Press
under the Breese Books imprint
for Baker Street Studios Ltd
Endeavour House
170 Woodland Road, Sawston
Cambridge, CB22 3DX, UK

ISBN: 1-901091-45-7 (10 digit)
ISBN: 978-1-901091-45-8 (13 digit)

Cover Concept: Antony J. Richards

Cover Illustration: Dr. Crippen outside the infamous 39 Hilldrop
Crescent, in the London Borough of Islington, from an original
watercolour by Nikki Sims.

Typeset in 8/11/20pt Palatino

About the Authors

During his life Val Andrews wrote over thirty new Sherlock Holmes adventures and was always at his best when writing about the world of entertainment, in which he worked as a writer and performer for fifty years. From a theatrical background, he had been in his time a professional vaudeville artiste, ventriloquist, magician and scriptwriter to Tommy Cooper, Benny Hill and other comedy legends of stage and television. He could even count among his friends the likes of Orson Welles.

Val Andrews was born in Hove near Brighton on the 15th February 1926 only a few hours after Valentine's Day and hence his Christian name. He was the son of an architect and indeed it was his father who introduced him to magic, a fascination that was to last a lifetime and was to result many biographies on the great magicians and numerous writings on magic in general.

He died from a heart attack on the 12th October 2006 and will be missed, but at least his name will live on through his books that continue to thrill old and new murder mystery enthusiasts alike.

David James Smith was born in south London and has been a journalist all his working life. His definitive account of the James Bulger case, *The Sleep of Reason* was published in 1994 by Century, Random House. He wrote for the monthly magazine *Esquire* before joining the *Sunday Times Magazine* for whom he has travelled around the world writing cover stories, investigative articles, reportage and profiles. It was an article for the *Magazine* that led to his second book, *All About Jill: The Life and Death of Jill Dando*, which was published by Little Brown in 2002. *Supper with the Crippens*, about the notorious Edwardian crime, was highly acclaimed when it was published by Orion in 2005. *One Morning in Sarajevo* made a gripping non-fiction thriller out of the assassination of Archduke Ferdinand in June, 1914. It was published by Weidenfeld & Nicholson in June, 2008. David's latest book, *Young Mandela*, was published in the United Kingdom by Weidenfeld in June 2010. He continues to write for the *Sunday Times Magazine* and has been a finalist several times in the feature writer of the year category at the British Press Awards. He lives in Lewes, East Sussex with his partner and their four children.

Introduction

David James Smith

There were one hundred and twenty executions by hanging at Pentonville Prison from the first at the turn of the twentieth century to the last in 1961.

The apparatus came from a familiar location, actually, from the old Newgate Prison that had been closed in 1902 to make way for the building of a new central criminal court on the same site – The Old Bailey.

The apparatus of the scaffold comprised a beam, cantilevered trap doors and a lever. They were installed in a purpose built suite of rooms in the exercise yard at Pentonville, just outside the prison B wing, which soon became known as the topping shed.

Hawley Harvey Crippen was executed there at nine o'clock in the morning on November 23rd, 1910. He had been convicted four weeks earlier of murdering his wife. His executioner, John Ellis described him as amiable ... gentlemanly ... a most pleasant fellow ...

So pleasant in fact that Ellis resolved to make his death as painless as possible, extending the length of the rope some inches beyond the established 'Table of Drops', a handy ready reckoner chart for hangings, which determined the length necessary according to the weight of the condemned man or woman, to make a clean break of the neck without decapitating them ... Ellis was keen on efficiency and always trying to cut down on the time it took to hang people. He counted sixty seconds between entering Crippen's cell and Crippen dropping through the trap doors to his death ... sixty seconds ... Ellis was especially proud of that.

Some people, even today, think that Crippen was wrongly convicted and should never have been hanged ... a posthumous pardon would do nicely. I fear they are being unduly optimistic, but let's look at the case together and see what you make of it ...

Crippen had gone to work as usual on February 1st 1910, following supper at home at thirty-nine Hilldrop Crescent, Camden with his wife and their friends the night before. A pot-luck supper was how Crippen had billed it to the other couple, Paul and Clara Martinetti. Not so lucky for his wife, however.

She had waved Paul and Clara into the night around one o'clock, never to be seen again.

Crippen worked in rooms at Albion House on New Oxford Street in various medical guises: Crippen and Rylance artificial teeth manufacturer ... the Yale Tooth Specialist manufacturer ... Munyon's Homeopathic Remedy Company ... he turned up there the day after his wife's disappearance, as if nothing had happened.

His wife, who often gets a bad press, quite unfairly in my view, was Belle Elmore a fizzing, spirited woman who was also the trusted and admired fund raiser and honorary treasurer of the Music Hall Ladies Guild. She had herself been a performer in mostly provincial halls. The Guild's offices were also in Albion House and its members were close friends and colleagues of Belle's.

How very puzzling for them, then, on Wednesday, February 2nd when Crippen's secretary Ethel le Neve handed the Guild two letters saying that Belle had been called away suddenly to America on urgent family business and was resigning her position.

Belle had never made such a trip before and how strange she had made no time, not even to say goodbye to any of her friends.

6

Ethel le Neve, it should be noted, was not just Crippen's secretary but also his lover. She never gave a formal statement to the police, and she never gave evidence in court. She only ever gave one press interview.

What she knew, and when she knew it, is worth bearing in mind as the story unfolds.

Ethel said that in one interview Crippen had told her Belle had finally left him. She gave the Crippen version of his life with Belle – that they were always on bad terms and she had often threatened to leave him.

This was the view that took hold as events progressed: Belle had extravagant tastes, a mean temper … she had affairs. She was a blousy, over ambitious, overbearing harridan and generally deserved what she got. It was really a wonder that Crippen, so quiet and reserved and uncomplaining himself, hadn't killed her sooner!

Ethel said Crippen gave her a handful of jewels from his pocket and told her to pick some … she chose a starburst brooch that was to become a famous emblem of the case. The Lord Chief Justice, sitting on the bench in the Old Bailey's Court Number One months later at Crippen's trial would describe it as 'a sort of star gentlemen, with apparent brilliants'.

That same day Crippen pawned several pieces of his wife's jewellery at a pawnbroker on Oxford Street returning with even more a week later.

In the days following her disappearance Crippen began telling different versions of the reason Belle had gone and soon started sowing the seeds for news of her demise with accounts of how she had fallen ill during the journey across the Atlantic …

On February 20th he made a terrible tactical blunder and turned up at the Music Hall Ladies Guild Ball with Ethel. She was wearing a pink dress that many at the dance thought must be one of Belle's, though in fact Ethel had bought it herself from Swan & Edgars on Piccadilly Circus.

The brooch pinned to the dress however was definitely, undeniably Belle's. Oh dear! Everyone recognised the starburst design and that set tongues wagging. What was going on between Crippen and his secretary, and where **was** his wife?

Belle's friends largely ignored Ethel at the Ball. Belle used to refer to her as the little typist. Being ignored must have been hard for Ethel. She had told her landlady in her digs in Hampstead that she was staying out the night before the Ball with Clara Martinetti who was doing her hair. I fancy that poignant lie betrays Ethel's social ambitions to escape her station and her ideal of the life she might lead as the next Mrs. Crippen.

That would have made her the third Mrs. Crippen. The first, Charlotte Bell had died in 1892 in the American state of Utah. Her cause of death was stated as apoplexy during childbirth. Crippen was there when it happened but returned afterwards to New York where he soon met Belle and married her seven months later on September 1st, 1892.

He was already thirty and she was just nineteen. Belle's father was Polish and her real name was Kunigunde Mackamotski. She had one sister, Theresa and a stepfather Frederick Mersinger who married her mother after her natural father died.

Not long after her marriage Belle had an operation to remove her ovaries and her womb meaning of course that she could not have children. In later life she sometimes showed off to friends the large scar the operation had left on her abdomen.

Crippen who was born in Michigan was indeed a properly qualified doctor, strangely drawn to the current vogue for homeopathic remedies. He had travelled widely in America before coming to London at the turn of the century to open the first European office of Munyon's, leaving behind one son Otto who grew up with his grandmother in California.

Crippen's new wife came with him to London. Belle had nursed ambitions to become an opera singer but ended up on the music hall circuit instead, with very, **very** modest success. A friend of hers, a writer once described her as a 'brilliant chattering bird of enormous plumage'.

Belle may have had one affair, with Bruce Miller a one-man band performer from Chicago who she met over dinner at the home of her voice coach in Bloomsbury while Crippen was in America on business. Miller sent letters to Belle that he signed, all very friendly, 'love and kisses to brown eyes'. But he denied in court ever having done more than kiss her. Crippen said that he and Belle had continued living together on his return but no longer as man and wife. They agreed to keep up appearances in front of friends, he said. But this was Crippen's evidence alone and had no corroboration. Belle's writer friend said Crippen idolised Belle and showered her with the gifts she craved of gowns, furs and jewellery.

Meanwhile his business career was checkered. New enterprises opened and closed with some regularity. He concocted remedies and tried to market them through mail order. It was not a particularly respectable or lucrative line of work. He was a properly qualified doctor, but he behaved like a quack.

The Crippens moved to thirty-nine Hilldrop Crescent in Camden in 1905, paying rent on a long lease. It was around this time that Belle told a friend she did not much like her husband's little typist, Ethel Le Neve. "Why don't you ask him to get rid of her then?" said the friend. "I have", said Belle, "but he told me she is indispensable."

Ethel was in her early twenties, born and bred to a poor rural family in Diss, Norfolk. Her father took the family off to London and seems to have shared some of the social aspirations shown by his daughter. It was he who initially changed his name from common or garden Neave to the more exotic and glamorous sounding Le Neve. Ethel was the first born of six children and it was her sister Adine True Neave who first went to work for Crippen, joined soon after by her sickly, neurotic sister Ethel. Adine left to be married. Ethel began an affair with her boss. They had quiet lunches at Frascatis, an Italian restaurant on Oxford Street and spent afternoons and evenings in rented rooms off Tottenham Court Road, becoming lovers or, as they would have said, becoming 'hub and wifey' to each other.

9

In the middle of January 1910 a full two weeks before the disappearance of the incumbent Mrs. Crippen, Ethel showed remarkable prescience in telling a friend she 'was engaged to be married to Dr. Crippen'.

This damming indicator of prior knowledge turned up in a bundle of unused case papers in the National Archives. No one appeared to have looked at them for nearly one hundred years before I stumbled across them during my research. They had formed no part of the court case. The papers contain witness statements that reveal the many, many lies Ethel told and suggest a far greater complicity than was ever suspected at the time.

By an even greater coincidence, at exactly the same time, on January 17th, Crippen ordered the poison he used to kill his wife: five grains of hyoscine from the chemist Lewis & Burrows at number one-hundred-and-eight New Oxford Street.

It was such a big request it had to be ordered in from the supplier. Crippen collected it two days later. Did he have malice aforethought? Probably ... yes ... and Ethel? What do you think?

Crippen finally announced Belle's death in California in March and declared he was going to France to recuperate. He failed to mention he was going off to a hotel in Dieppe with Ethel who, bizarrely, told her sister and select friends the trip was in fact her honeymoon and that she and Crippen were now married ... 'We've been and gone and done it', she wrote excitedly in a postcard.

Complete nonsense, of course. There was no wedding, as Ethel well knew. What was she thinking of? Back in Hilldrop Crescent she started behaving like the mistress of the house, generously giving Belle's clothes away to her own family and friends, even hiring a French maid to **do** for her.

Just imagine, if you can, taking over the clothes, the jewellery, and the life of your husband's ex-wife who had so recently been de-boned and buried beneath the floor bricks of the coal cellar, with or without your knowledge.

After their Dieppe expedition, Crippen and Ethel started going about openly as if they really were 'hub and wifey'. The Ladies Guild members were becoming increasingly suspicious now, and started to question Crippen about exactly what had happened to Belle.

His attempts to fend them off only resulted in him digging himself in deeper with more lies. They called at his home and called again when there was no answer. They pressed him for the name of the ship Belle had travelled on. One of them hired an investigator. They wrote to Crippen's son Otto in Los Angeles and he wrote back saying he knew nothing about it.

By now all Belle's friends believed Crippen was lying. John and Lilian Nash – she was Lil Hawthorne a star of the music hall – made one last attempt to question him at the end of June and then went straight to Scotland Yard. Inspector Walter Dew, a veteran of the 'Jack the Ripper' murder investigations from two decades ago was assigned to make inquiries.

Dew and a sergeant went to Hilldrop Crescent and found Ethel who took the officers to Albion House ... the three of them travelling together on the bus.

Dew questioned Crippen in his office for several hours, only breaking to go with him to lunch at the Holborn Restaurant. Dew observed later how Crippen ate his lunch like a man without a care in the world. How often, I wonder, has a detective gone to lunch with his murder suspect.

Crippen told him that, actually, he had lied to Belle's friends, but only out of embarrassment – she was not dead, she had run off to her lover in Chicago.

Ethel told Dew her family thought she was the housekeeper at Hilldrop. Well that was another outrageous lie as she had told her family she was now Mrs. Crippen. Of course she could not tell Dew about that, now that Crippen was saying Belle was still alive after all. What an extraordinary mosaic of lies and double lies. The two officers went back to Hilldrop Crescent with Crippen and Ethel and made a cursory search of the house ... of course failing to find the body ... not a great moment, you may think, in the annals of Scotland Yard.

Crippen and Ethel must have known their lies would soon be exposed. They decided that night to cut and run and fled the following morning after first going to the office where Crippen cut Ethel's hair into a boyish look and prepared her disguise as his son, wearing clothes Crippen sent his assistant to buy from a nearby menswear store. The trousers had to be gathered in with safety pins.

They took the train to Harwich and the night boat to the Hook of Holland. They were in Rotterdam after breakfast the next day and moved on to Brussels where they remained for eight nights at the Hotel des Ardennes as John Robinson of Quebec and his mute son Master Robinson, aged sixteen.

Dew resumed his inquiries on Monday morning July 11th, 1910. Over the next forty-eight hours, he and his sergeant returned to Albion House where they learned that Crippen had disappeared. They went to the house and found that empty too. They searched high and low throughout and finally began prodding at the cellar floor with a poker.

A brick moved ... and then another. It was around five o'clock on Wednesday July 13th, 1910. The smell of the exposed remains was rank and overpowering. Fortunately, the Metropolitan Police assistant commissioner turned up with a handful of strong cigars for his officers to smoke. A constable was dispatched to buy some disinfectant that they liberally sloshed around. No worries back then about contaminating a crime scene ... or smoking indoors.

They lifted out the remains by hand and placed them in a metal bucket where they were examined by the police surgeon, Thomas Marshall, who also conducted the post mortem with a consultant surgeon from St. Mary's Hospital, one Augustus Pepper.

The remains were left exposed on a mortuary slab for five days ... sprinkled with carbolic powder and covered with brown paper.

There were no limbs or bones among the remains and no genitalia. In fact it was hard to say if they were male or female, though among the pieces of skin were a tuft of hair in a Hindes curler, two more curlers, some more tufts of hair and pieces of women's underwear and, famously, a piece of a pyjama top bearing the label Jones Brothers, a department store on the Holloway Road.

All the internal organs were there, all except the ovaries and the uterus – the two things you will recall that Belle had lost during surgery. One piece of flesh had a mark that Pepper concluded was the scar of an old operation. He and Marshall agreed the dismemberment had been conducted with a surgeon's skill.

The hue and cry went up.

The story of the discovery at Hilldrop Crescent and the suspects' flight quickly travelled across the developed world. It was, as Damon Runyon might have said 'more than somewhat embarrassing to Scotland Yard and in particular Inspector Dew that he had allowed Crippen to escape, especially after they had lunched together'.

He was the subject of much public criticism and ridicule, even in parliament. But he was lucky. On July 22nd a Marconigram arrived from a Captain Kendall, the commander of the SS Montrose, a passenger ship on its way from Europe to Canada … 'Have strong suspicion that Crippen, London cellar murderer and accomplice are among saloon passengers'.

The Marconigram system was only three years old and few ships had use of it. The SS Montrose was at the cutting edge of new technology. No murderer had ever yet been caught by such newfangled means.

Even so, Dew could not contact the ship and had no way of confirming the sighting but he and his superiors decided it was a chance worth taking. He boarded a faster ship, the SS Laurentic, also bound for Canada. He travelled under a pseudonym but was soon rumbled by the press who also set off in pursuit, tracking the drama with maps and charts in their daily newspapers.

Kendall would say later he was suspicious from the start, when he saw Ethel squeezing Crippen's hand tightly on deck. After that he watched them carefully and engaged Crippen in conversation to keep him close and untroubled.

On Sunday morning, July 31st as the ship neared Quebec, Ethel lay reading romantic fiction in her room and Crippen was up on deck, while a pilot came aboard and went straight to the captain's cabin. Two men came to Crippen and invited him to the cabin too. The pilot was Inspector Dew in disguise. "Good morning Dr. Crippen," he said. "Good morning," said Crippen calmly. Ethel swooned when she was arrested in her cabin. Crippen said, "it is only fair to say she knows nothing about it. I never told her anything."

Anything about what?

The anxiety, he said, had been too awful.

We always say that Crippen never admitted his guilt, but those words are pretty damn close to a confession. Both he and Ethel were the very model of perfect prisoners. Crippen was already well on his way to becoming the 'mild mannered murderer', such a decent courteous, considerate little man so cruelly mistreated by his wife. That assessment of him left little cause for concern at his cool dismembering and filleting of that same wife.

Ethel's caricature was of the naive, innocent secretary blinded by her love for her boss. That was another myth that did not stand up to scrutiny.

They returned to Liverpool by steamship and took the train to London where they fought through mobs and appeared at Bow Street Police Court, photographed side by side in the dock by a pressman with a camera hidden in his hat. Court photography was discouraged, but not then illegal. It was only outlawed in 1925.

Ethel went to Holloway Prison and Crippen to Brixton Prison. Everywhere they went crowds of hundreds followed and newspapers devoted acres of coverage to the case.

The Times thundered in a leading article about this new and vulgar curiosity, calling it a 'besetting sin of the age'. The leader said, 'They flock to see a murderer because murder is a crime that appals them ... because they have a human interest in the extremes of human nature ... but their imagination like their curiosity is passive'.

Not for the first time, and certainly not the last, *The Times* was splendidly unashamed of its own hypocrisy, devoting entire broadsheet pages to the case while complaining about the kinds of people who wanted to read it.

Like Crippen, Ethel was initially accused of murder but that charge was dropped by the time of the committal proceedings a week later and she was instead arraigned as being an accessory.

She and Crippen shared the same solicitor ... the word dodgy might have been invented for him. His name was Arthur Newton and he would eventually end up in prison himself, convicted of fraud, and was clearly a self-interested character with an eye to the main chance. He had been quick off the mark in writing to Crippen offering his legal services while Crippen was still in Canada.

Back in London, Newton used the ruse of Legal Conferences with his client in Brixton Prison as a cover to take notes for a life story of Crippen that he planned to sell to pay his fees, in those days before legal aid.

The Home Secretary, one Winston Churchill, had taken a close personal interest in the Crippen saga and was furious when he heard what Newton was up to, but did point out that it would be hard to further aggravate the scales of publicity and sensationalism surrounding the case.

The committal sailed through and the trial was set for October. The Director of Public Prosecutions, Sir Charles Matthews, appointed Treasury Counsel Richard Muir to lead the prosecution supported by Travers Humphreys and S. Ingleby Oddie. Muir was a workaholic who kept his team in long consultations every night through the trial. From the start he and Humphreys complained about the role of the police, feeling they should never have allowed Crippen to escape in the first place. Half the country thought that too, of course.

But, far from being determined to make amends, Dew seemed, as Muir put it, to be suffering from 'sleepy sickness'.

Instead it was Muir himself who drove the quest for crucial answers that might bolster an otherwise circumstantial case. He hoped they might be able to date the Jones Brothers pyjama top, and so counter the inevitable defence argument that the remains were already there when the Crippens moved in to Hilldrop Crescent and Belle was in fact still alive. It was not until just a week before the trial was due to start that the prosecution decided against putting Ethel in the dock alongside Crippen. They feared a jury sympathetic to Ethel might be sympathetic to Crippen too and end up acquitting them both. Richard Muir went further, indicating that he would offer no case against Ethel as an accessory to murder. The details are recorded on a memo in the National Archives. It was clear that only Crippen mattered. Ethel's legal fate was of little importance. How fortunate she was. I feel strongly that, with a little investigative effort, she would have hanged too.

The glamorous young politician and barrister F. E. Smith, Lord Birkenhead, was offered Crippen's defence but turned it down and took Ethel's instead. Some of his colleagues were sniffy about this ambitious upstart and suspected he had rejected Crippen because it was a case that could not be won, whereas Ethel would be easy to defend.

The solicitor Arthur Newton had worked with the celebrated criminal barrister Edward Marshall Hall on the 1907 Camden Town murders, later depicted in paintings by Walter Sickert. Hall had secured an acquittal against the odds in that case and seemed the obvious choice for Crippen's defence, but rejected it, apparently after a row over the size of his fee. The defence brief went instead to Sir Alfred Tobin who did little with not very much. Newton seems to have spent more time selling Crippen than he did defending him. A lost cause from the start.

As I suppose one or two of you may already know, in 1910 the Central Criminal Court was still very much the new Old Bailey, having opened for business just three years earlier. Until 1860 executions were held there in public, in the street just outside Newgate Prison with so called 'hanging

16

breakfasts', an early form of corporate hospitality held in the overlooking rooms, where the food and the wine were plentiful for those who could afford it, while the riff raff of London filled out the street around the scaffold, a crush of many, many hundreds often resulting in deaths and injuries.

A photograph of that same street on the opening day of the Crippen trial, October 18th, 1910 shows that the same numbers had returned for this new spectacle, which remains an unparalleled event in the history of the court. I do not believe that any case since has attracted such overwhelming interest. There were five thousand applications for seats in the public gallery. Corporation of London officials decided to split the viewing day in half to accommodate as many people as possible. Red tickets for the mornings, and blue tickets for the afternoons.

The jury was all male. Women were not allowed to be jurors until 1921. One of the few women in court was a noted actress of the day, Phyllis Dare, a mere spectator whose presence must have so pleased the judge that he allowed her to sit next to him, for the duration of her visit – perhaps more than usually, you may feel, blurring the narrow distinction between the criminal court and the theatre.

Crippen was photographed sitting in the dock, the angle clearly betraying the photographer's position in the public gallery. Crippen looks a very lonely, isolated figure in that picture.

Muir's opening speech offered two motives for the crime – that of money – Belle had a substantial sum on deposit – and Crippen's desire to get her out of the way so that he could be with his mistress, Ethel Le Neve.

It was the expert evidence in the case that fascinated. It was the Home Office forensic scientist, Dr. William Willcox, who had found the poison hyoscine in Belle's remains and testified to its power as a narcotic that could cause delirium and death. He found half a grain in the remains, more than twice the fatal dose. Crippen you may remember had purchased five grains. There was none left. He was unable to account for any of it, and had no records to show it had been used to treat his clients.

The defence had an expert, Dr. Blyth, who had written a book on poisons and appeared ready to say Willcox had been mistaken in identifying hyoscine in the remains. But he was very quickly tied up in knots by Richard Muir as his evidence contradicted his own book.

The defence struggled with its medical experts especially at the heart of the battle between the two sides, with the prosecution's determination to prove the remains must have been those of Belle, and the defence efforts to sow seeds of doubt, and suggest they could have belonged to someone else.

The Crown had three experts all saying the mark on the largest piece of flesh was the scar of an operation. They included the young pathologist Bernard Spilsbury who was just thirty-three and ruffling older feathers with his youthful zeal.

The defence thought it could argue the mark was in fact a simple fold – but there was already a fold next to the mark the prosecution said was a scar and it was plainly separate from it. One oddity was the absence of a navel on the skin fragment – it ought to have been there. The Crown said it could have been removed during Belle's operation. The defence was not helped when its main medical witness, Dr. Turnbull, claimed to have been tricked into giving evidence by the solicitor Arthur Newton after they had met at a bridge party.

Poor Turnbull had signed a report saying the scar was a fold and was now forced to defend that implausible position in the witness box, in the full glare of the trial of the century. His interrogation by Muir was humiliating and made him look a fool, the more so as he had tried to come out fighting. In the end he told the court that he had been promised he would never have to give evidence, if he signed a report saying the scar was a fold. His inspection of the piece of skin, the piece that was scarred or folded or both, he admitted, had lasted just twenty minutes.

18

Crippen's case as outlined by Tobin slowly crumbled around him. He had promised to call evidence that the remains had been in the cellar longer than five years but no such evidence was ever actually called.

All the witnesses agreed that Crippen was kind-hearted, goodhearted ... decent. All Tobin had was unsubstantiated, empty rhetoric: Where was Belle now? Who could say she had not run off? Who knew for certain she was not still out there alive somewhere?

Crippen said he had no idea whose remains were in the cellar. He knew nothing about them, he said, until he got back to London after his arrest in Canada. His cross-examination began at the start of the fourth day of the trial, October 21st, 1910. It was a brilliant and devastating opening volley from Richard Muir.

"On the morning of the first of February you were left alone in your house with your wife?"
"Yes."
"She was alive?"
"Yes."
"Do you know of any person in the world who has seen her alive since?"
"I do not."

He assumed she was in America with Bruce Miller but had made no inquiries as to her whereabouts, not even since his arrest.

Crippen disclosed that Ethel had stayed with him at the house the following night. The information was never used against Ethel but how could she not have known. Crippen himself went to work that first day. Belle must have taken an age to cut up and fillet and dispose of, possibly by fire. Ethel just must have been in on it.

Muir made the most of the many lies Crippen had told, pretending to be the bereaved husband when, so he claimed, he knew all along she had run off to her one-man band lover in Chicago. He could not of course explain the remains, perhaps someone else had put them there while he and his

19

wife were out, he said feebly. Perhaps they were already there. This opened the door for the rebuttal evidence of the pyjama jacket that, Muir could now demonstrate, came from cloth made in late 1908. There was even a receipt for their purchase by Belle on January 5th 1909: three pairs in all priced seventeen shillings and nine pence.

The closing speeches did nothing to alter Crippen's fate. The Lord Chief Justice in his summing up reminded the jury they were not in a court of morals but a court of law. 'The immorality of the victim and of the accused might be a matter of regret but were no reason to convict, or to acquit ...'

He was kind to Belle describing her as 'beautifully dressed ... spick and span ... if she really had gone away why had she not taken her clothes, furs and jewellery?'

The jury went out on Saturday afternoon on day five of the trial and came back twenty-seven minutes later to find Crippen guilty of wilful murder.

The defendant was standing in the dock. Did he have anything to say? He did. "I still protest my innocence," he said.

May the Lord have mercy on his soul.

He was hanged at Pentonville Prison on November 23rd, 1910.

As you may have read or seen on television in recent times, an American forensic scientist provided with one of Bernard Spilsbury's original slides of the scar tissue has tested for DNA and claims to have found it contains not female but male DNA. He has compared it with the DNA of two alleged descendants of Belle's family and concluded they do not match.

I have read the report of that scientist and only wish I could put him in that witness box and cross-examine him. But I can't. I'm not a lawyer for a start.

I can only tell you that Crippen killed his wife beyond any shadow of a doubt and the hair curlers, the hyoscine, the scar tissue, the pyjama top, the mysterious way in which Belle was there one minute and gone the next, vanished off the face of the earth, the many lies of her husband and his lover, the affair between 'hub and wifey', their flight, his near admission on arrest all point to the inexorable conclusion that the right verdict was reached, and the right man hanged.

I am far more inclined to take issue with the verdict in Ethel's trial. She was acquitted in a day with little effort expended to mount a compelling case against her. She disappeared from view immediately after the trial and was variously said to have started a new life in Canada, Australia and various places in between.

In fact, as I discovered, Ethel did briefly go to Canada but didn't like it there and came home again to London where she lived out her days in almost total anonymity. Poignantly she took the surname Harvey after her hanged lover. That was the name she signed with on the day of her marriage to a clerk named Smith. They had two children together and were long married. Mr. Smith died never knowing his wife was the notorious Ethel Le Neve. She died aged eighty-four in 1967 without ever telling her two children either. They only found out later. As you can imagine, it was quite a shock.

Ethel had only one confidante, a friend named Rex to whom, on her death she bequeathed a fob watch, the same watch worn by Crippen and returned to her among his possessions after the execution.

I am not especially a romantic but I do believe that the letters exchanged by Crippen and Ethel to and from the condemned cell betray a profound love, perhaps heightened by the extreme circumstances in which they were written.

I have no doubt that Crippen took his secrets to the scaffold to protect his lover's involvement. I am sure he killed Belle to get to Ethel. I know that is why Belle died. What I cannot tell you is precisely how she died or what happened to the rest of her remains. That mystery, I suspect, finally died with Ethel and can never now be solved.

Supper with the Crippens

'David James Smith, a journalist, has been meticulous in his research and this book is likely to remain the definitive account of a crime which still intrigues, and to an extent baffles, aficionados of murder.' (Review by P. D. James in the *Sunday Telegraph*)

David James Smith has uncovered substantial fresh evidence that explodes popular myths surrounding this notorious crime. Here for the first time is the truth of the case: a dark, psychological drama in which class and desire and social ambition become powerful motives for murder, and the popular belief in a young woman's innocence of the crime is destroyed.

ISBN: 978-0752867427, 352 pages, Hardcover, Orion (2005).

Available from all good bookshops.
Also see David James Smith's own web site for more
information on this and his other works:
www.davidjamessmith.net

Chapter One

A Day Out With Sherlock Holmes

It was in the spring of 1911 that I found myself at Victoria Station, responding to a telegram from Sherlock Holmes. After seven years of his bee-keeping exile in Fowlhaven I doubted very much if this meant that the game was afoot; indeed I was intrigued by the brevity of his message and the short notice that it had given me.

"Watson, my dear fellow it is good to see you again. How long has it been?"

"It must be a year, or even more!"

As we made for the refreshment room at Victoria Station with its imposing marble columns and tables topped with the same material, I was glad to notice that he seemed to be in good health and spirits. Dressed in a neat town suit and broad-brimmed black hat, he didn't look like a countryman up for the day. He carried a Gladstone and a waterproof was draped over his arm. We sat in an alcove, near the entrance at the opposite end from the one through which we had entered. The waitress had soon set individual coffee pots before us and Holmes sat back in his seat, seemingly relaxed.

"Most of my time is spent in gratitude for the peace and harmony – only provided by the Sussex countryside Watson, but once in a while I suddenly yearn for the bustle and noise of the big city. Such a feeling came upon me last evening, hence the presence of your humble servant."

I have never been able to think of Sherlock Holmes either as humble or servile but did not, of course, say as much. Instead I made enquiries regarding his immediate plans. He was irritatingly vague in his reply. "I may stay at the Station Hotel, at Charing Cross, for a day or two, a week even, it depends ..."

He did not tell me upon what it depended and I did not ask him. Instead I waited for his next words as I noted that the weather in the country had toned the complexion of his pronounced cheekbones and aquiline nose giving him something of the style of a North American Indian. I had hoped that he might become a little more forthcoming over his coffee or in the taxicab, which took us to Charing Cross, but it was not so, for he simply peered out of the window as we passed the landmarks so familiar to us both with renewed interest. However, the journey was short and I thought perhaps as we relaxed in the hotel lounge that he might give me some clue as to his plans. It was not until we were walking in the Strand that he began to be more open in his manner.

"So many years I resided in this huge metropolis Watson without really doing more than take it all for granted. You realise that visitors come here from all over the world to take in and experience London? Why ever when I first arrived here, so many years ago, I only allowed myself a few days to become acclimatised." I heard his words but could not quite believe that Sherlock Holmes wished to spend a few days in London sightseeing!

We started by taking a stroll with Holmes assuming automatically in his usual cavalier fashion that I could change all of my own arrangements. He was as irritating and condescending as ever but he was still the best and wisest man I had ever known and it was as always a pleasure to be in his company. He looked keenly and with renewed interest at all he saw in the park; the squirrels, the nursemaids with their perambulators and strolling couples and, without even consulting me, handed the man in charge of the turnstile of the Zoological Gardens some coins so that we could both enter. As we passed the huge bovines just inside the entrance and wandered up the broad walk and then dawdled before the row of imprisoned birds of prey, he reflected upon how few visits I had made to the zoo. I knew that Holmes had spent quite a lot of his time in the menagerie through the years, though usually when pursuing some enigma with some natural history connection.

After walking through the reverberating tunnel, shrill with the screams of children who had discovered the echo, we gained the north gardens and were soon surveying the elephants. Our eyes lighted upon their vast grey shapes. There were both African and Asiatic specimens on view, the latter, bolder than their cousins shot insinuating trunks through the railings of their enclosure, like gross pickpockets exploring possibilities. But the African specimens drew Holmes's attention and he said, "Do they not remind you of Barnum's Jumbo which figured in one of my earliest cases?"

I remembered well the riddle of the missing elephant that the Zoological Society had sold to the great American showman. Surely only Sherlock Holmes could have explained how a four ton elephant could disappear from the gardens and be missing without a trace!

We made our exit through the north gate and walked down the hill and into Camden Town. A cab took us on the short journey to Holmes's next desired port of call that turned out to be the waxwork exhibition of Madame Tussaud. It was so near to our old rooms at Baker Street, yet I had to admit that I had not visited the exhibition in many years. Possibly Holmes had never visited it and I enquired of him if this was so. He replied, "But once Watson, back in the days when it was still little more than an enlarged fairground side show. But now, I am assured, it is of a rather more sophisticated nature."

This proved to be so, for no tented enterprise could have used the novelties recently possible through scientific discovery. The electric light had been cleverly utilised, as had various means of theatrical effect. Indeed, in some cases, the combination of the lighting transforms one scene and set of figures into another. The mixed odours of wax, fabrics, and scene-painters size gave an exciting back stage atmosphere to the whole place. We passed rather quickly through the historical section where classic portraits had obviously influenced the models of kings, queens and nobles both famous and infamous. The section that displayed the guillotine and heads of decapitated French aristocrats slowed Holmes's pace a little. I remembered, as Holmes obviously did, the story of the young Madame Tussaud forced, on pain of death, to use her modelling skills in making moulds of the grisly heads. He remarked, as ever reading my mind, "But fate was also kind in allowing her to escape with those moulds which enabled her to start her exhibition."

In the hall of the celebrated I knew that my friend fully took in the representations of ourselves even though he appeared not to have even given the two figures a glance. I knew because later he remarked to me that the replication of the living room at 221B had been quite detailed. He was right, for everything seemed to be there, including the V.R. bullet scars, the Turkish slipper, the chemistry bench and the shelves of albums and reference volumes. Holmes was well captured in wax, even if the crimson dressing robe was a little too new. The less said concerning the representation of myself the better!

As we walked past Maskelyne and Devant, Marconi, Eddison, Irving, George Robey and Marie Lloyd the path led us into the hall of the infamous rather than the celebrated. Burke and Hare were depicted disinterring a corpse, Laundru suffocating a victim, Jack the Ripper attacking an unfortunate female and eventually the figure of the bespectacled and downtrodden looking Dr. Crippen, standing in the dock of the Old Bailey. The fact that Crippen had been hanged but sixteen weeks earlier showed how alert to topicality were the current organisers of the Madame Tussaud exhibition. Holmes stopped to read the details of the infamous murder case displayed beside this exhibit. They were scant in detail.

We had been able to enter the building without having to wait, but now, as we left, we noticed that a large crowd of people were waiting to gain entrance. As they stood there an itinerant salesman waved copies of a tract before them, shouting, "Read all about Crippen the murderer, the monster who robbed and killed his wife so that he could go off with the seductress, Ethel le Neve. For her delights he killed Belle Elmore, darling of the music halls! Only two pennies to read about the mad Dr. Crippen, Crippen the monster, Crippen the murderer!" His trade seemed quite brisk, and I was amazed to see Sherlock Holmes slip some coppers into his grubby hand and take a copy of the tract.

It was not until we had made a lightning visit to the Tower of London and were comfortably seated in Simpson's in the Strand that I mentioned the Crippen affair. "Surely Holmes you must have kept up with the Crippen case? Why even the yellow press must have published more accurate accounts of it than that which you purchased from that fellow?"

"Quite so Watson, but I did not follow the case beyond the merest glance at the headlines. You see during that time I was not only managing my hives but also helping a neighbour who was suffering at the hands of some extremely persistent and well organised poachers. The local police seemed unable to help and the fact that the wrongdoers were not simple yokels but an organised ring captured my interest. I was able to unmask the actual ringleaders but it took up a great deal of my time over a protracted period."

I was amazed, saying, "But Holmes, this after all your protestations that you would never ply your trade as a private consulting detective again!"

"Quite so Watson but I owed Fletcher a number of favours: you see it was he who helped me enormously during my first feeble attempts at setting up my swarm and hives. He also had advised me, even earlier, on the purchase of a suitable smallholding: and you know how ideal for my purposes my present situation is, not to mention the cottage that goes with the land?"

"I see, so your retirement is unaffected, in which case the current crime cases would scarcely interest you?"

Sherlock Holmes finished his dessert before he made further reply. But once he had lowered his fork he spoke warmly at some length. "My dear fellow, non-participation and lack of interest are two very different things. If you were not my best, nay, only friend I would say that you were trying to trap me into some sort of confession by your clever use of words. Surely old friend you could allow me to express interest in a criminal case which rather slipped through the fingers of my interest without further chastisement?"

"Why Holmes, do I chastise? I had no intention of doing so. Come, if it interests you to discuss the Crippen affair I am happy to do so. Aye, and to fill in with any detail of the business that I can remember."

Sherlock Holmes threw down his napkin and clapped his hands together, saying, "Spoken like a gentleman, a scholar and a good friend." He handed me the tract in question saying, "You have a gift of reading aloud in a most effective way. Might I persuade you to read the little document so that we can both absorb its contents with the minimum of delay?"

How could I refuse this diplomatic request? The following is a transcript of that text.

MURDER CASE OF THE CENTURY!
MARCONI AIDS IN BRINGING MONSTER TO JUSTICE!

The recently executed Doctor Hawley Crippen gained doubtful qualifications in America twenty-five years ago when working for a patent medicine firm. He returned to this country where he married a variety artiste, Belle Elmore and in the autumn of 1905 they moved into the house at 39 Hilldrop Crescent, Holloway, London, where she would later meet her untimely death at his hands. Later in his own defence

Crippen would claim that Belle, although a success on the music halls was very mean with her finances and treated him with disrespect on account of his small build which contrasted strangely with her own ample proportions. He claimed that it was her constant ridicule and close-fisted behaviour that drove him into the arms of his mistress, Ethel le Neve, who worked as a typist at his place of business.

In the middle of January 1910 Crippen collected five grains of hyoscine, a poison, from a chemist in New Oxford Street. In early February of the same year Crippen pawned some jewellery. Earlier still in the same month Crippen sent an apology for his wife's non-appearance at the Music Hall Ladies Guild. It was explained in the note that Belle had to go to America for a protracted stay and offered her resignation. Early in March Ethel moved into the house at Hilldrop Crescent. The couple went to France for the Easter holidays. When they returned, Crippen started to inform Belle's friends that she had died in America and had been cremated. Mr. and Mrs. Nash, close friends of Belle's, arrived back from America where they had been doing a vaudeville tour. They had enquired concerning Belle over there without success.

They were not happy with Crippen's story.

Nash consulted a Chief Inspector Dew of Scotland Yard who was a friend of his and asked him to investigate. The Inspector called upon Crippen who told him that he had invented the stories about the death of Belle to save himself from ridicule when she had left him for another name. Dew seemed satisfied with Crippen's story, but when he called again to ask more questions found that Crippen and Ethel had departed from the house, Crippen having sold his interest in the business to a partner.

Whilst at Hilldrop Crescent, Dew discovered some loose bricks in the cellar floor, beneath which he discovered signs of human remains; some flesh and some blonde hair. There were traces of hyoscine and this was enough for Dew to issue an arrest warrant for Crippen and le Neve.

On July 20th Captain Kendall, commander of the SS Montrose, sailing from Antwerp to Quebec noticed that two of his passengers, a Mr. Robinson and his son John, were behaving in a suspiciously affectionate manner toward each other and he radioed his observations to the ship's owners who contacted Scotland Yard. Dew was able to reach Quebec by a faster sea route and arrested the couple when they landed and brought them back to London.

Crippen's main defence at his trial, which opened on October 18th and lasted only four days, was that there was no proof that the remains in the cellar were those of his wife. The jury took only 27 minutes to find him guilty. Ethel's trial lasted only one day and she was acquitted.

John Ellis hanged Crippen at Pentonville Prison on November 23rd, 1910. For the first time ever the Marconi wire system resulted in a criminal being brought to justice. The wire was worded as follows ...

HAVE STRONG SUSPICIONS THAT LONDON CELLAR MURDERER CRIPPEN AND ACCOMPLICE ARE AMONGST SALOON PASSENGERS MOUSTACHE TAKEN OFF GROWING BEARD ACCOMPLICE DRESSED AS BOY VOICE MANNER AND BUILD UNDOUBTEDLY A GIRL TRAVELLING AS MR AND MASTER ROBINSON

KENDALL

Sir Bernard Spillsbury, the pathologist is to be congratulated upon being able to present the evidence that convicted Crippen from such scanty specimens of flesh and hair.

There followed various badly reproduced photographs of Crippen, Ethel le Neve and Belle Elmore. I returned the tract to Holmes and awaited his reaction but it was not until the waiter had brought our coffee and liqueurs that he made comment. Finally his words were in form of a question. "What do you make of it Watson?" I replied that I supposed it gave a fairly comprehensive summing up of the whole affair.

He did not altogether agree with me.

"Watson it is written in the absolute assumption that Crippen was guilty."

"You consider there is even the vaguest possibility that Crippen was innocent?"

"Considering the brevity of such a complex case and how scant the evidence was against him I think it extremely likely."

"What about the jury?"

"Exactly Watson, could you decide upon a man's life or death on such evidence in less than half an hour?"

I considered carefully before I replied that I felt it might be difficult, although of course I felt sure that rather more evidence must have been presented in court than mentioned in a two penny tract. Our dialogue continued as we strolled the short distance from Simpson's to the Charing Cross Hotel. Holmes seemed determined to be sceptical concerning the result of Crippen's trial saying, "No body was produced. The presentation of a body is important to the prosecution in English law is it not?"

"Why yes, but surely those portions of flesh, muscle and hair were sufficient to represent a body?"

"Even with strands of blonde female hair, assumed to be female on account of the signs of colouration, with a few

31

scraps of flesh and sinew were hardly enough to stand in place as a body, even though considered to be by such an eminent pathologist as Sir Bernard Spillsbury."

"You do not consider then, Holmes, that Crippen was guilty of the murder?"

"I did not say that Watson, I just feel that his trial was somewhat suspect."

"Surely Crippen was revealed to be a really shady character?"

"You suggest then Watson that all shady characters should be hanged by the neck until dead?"

"No, I just think that he was unworthy of your concern, especially as you have yourself admitted that a miscarriage of justice is only a vague possibility."

I sincerely hoped that Holmes would shortly drop the entire subject. After all, guilty or innocent, Crippen had been executed. I searched my mind for some diversion to take his mind from the topic. As we entered the hotel and repaired to the coffee lounge, I was relieved to see the seated figure of George Lestrade, the ex-Scotland Yard Detective Inspector, who had shared so many adventures with Holmes and myself during those halcyon days when the rooms at Baker Street had figured so often in his itinerary. He rose, standing only very slightly bowed from age, and greeted us both in his same old manner of crusty good humour. "Mr. Holmes, Dr. Watson, it is nice to see you both again. When I received your telegram I dropped everything, including even building a new shed in the garden, to join you."

I noted that he still had that ironic tone in his words. I knew that he had been long retired; longer even than Holmes himself, from active crime investigation. I sensed that this meeting was saving both of them from expiring through boredom! Holmes smiled and shook Lestrade warmly by the hand. "I apologise for the lateness of this arranged meeting, but my time in London may be short and I may return to Sussex on the morrow."

"So you and the Doctor must have found a great deal to talk about, for I know that you do not meet that often."

I said, "Holmes has rushed me off my feet Lestrade, we have today visited the Zoological Gardens, Madame Tussaud's and the Tower of London."

"So you have been behaving like a couple of tourists then Doctor; seeing the sights as it were."

Holmes said, with mock severity, "Hardly my dear Lestrade, few tourists can claim to have retrieved a missing elephant or prevented the theft of the crown jewels. I enjoyed revisiting the sites of these exploits as I am sure you would have too; for you were involved yourself in both of these adventures if you remember?"

"Mr. Holmes I am unlikely to forget Barnum's pachyderm or yet your impersonation of Sir William Gillette's impersonation of yourself! Yet I fail to recall a case of yours which involved the old lady's waxwork show."

"Your memory is not at fault Lestrade, but neither Watson nor I had visited her establishment for many a long year."

By this time of course we had been seated comfortably for some minutes and neither of them had shown any sign of calling a waiter so I took the law into my own hands so to speak and ordered a pot of tea and one of coffee.

Holmes broke the silence that had occurred only that we might pour tea or coffee. "Whilst at the exhibition we saw the effigy of Crippen, the so-called murderer. The old lady's descendants are as enterprising as she was herself." His words of doubt caused Lestrade to start a little and he enquired, "You consider there was the possibility of a miscarriage of justice?" Holmes said that he thought there was a vague possibility and to my very great surprise Lestrade nodded wisely. My heart sank for I knew now that a topic of conversation that I could have well done without was about to recommence!

Sherlock Holmes laid before our friend all those doubts that he had shared with me including his misgivings concerning the way that the justice system had operated. Again to my amazement Lestrade nodded at almost every view that Holmes opined.

Then he asked, "Mr. Holmes, why did you not make some kind of a protest at the trial?"

"It is rare for me to be out of touch with current affairs even isolated as I am in Fowlhaven. The truth is, as I have already explained to Watson, I was for some weeks completely absorbed with the problems of a good neighbour. But you Lestrade, you were on the spot, known and respected by the authorities. Why did you not yourself protest?"

Lestrade lit a small cigar before he replied, "Do you suppose that I did not try? So much so that I'm afraid I made a nuisance of myself and although no direct threat was made the modest stipend that my many years with the force have entitled me to was pointedly mentioned. I understood only too well that I must mind my own business or face actual threats."

Holmes's brows knitted with anger. He too smoked a cigar when I know that he would have preferred to fill the hotel coffee lounge with fumes produced by the Scottish mixture. He responded, "But I do not share your vulnerability Lestrade, though I realise that I would be extended little more co-operation than your good self. But there is nothing to stop me investigating the whole affair from scratch."

I had not interrupted their exchanges for some time but felt that I should make some token protest to prevent Sherlock Holmes from wasting his time upon a lost cause. I said, "I know I am a man of science, but in the company of you both I am a mere layman concerning crime and the law. Yet even I know that another trial is not only near impossible to achieve but useless as Crippen is already dead."

Lestrade said, "Doctor, with the greatest respect, if he was innocent this should go on record as being so. If Mr. Holmes were able to prove his innocence it would not be immediately accepted. But in the fullness of time when the present powers that be at the Yard are dead and gone the doubt would be taken up."

Holmes added, "Lestrade is right Watson; I am by no means sure that an injustice has been done, but I hate to see shoddy work, and that is what I am forced to believe there has been. If Crippen was guilty we can put our minds at rest by proving it. If not, it is my duty to at least establish my findings." Inattention to his cigar had caused it to extinguish itself, he re-lit it with a Vesta before he continued, "In any case Watson, it would be exhilarating for the game to be afoot once more. I enjoy the tranquillity of my present abode, and I would not, I believe, go back on my word to never again become professionally engaged in criminal investigation but, well, I just need to know that my mind has lost none of its cunning and this seems a good opportunity."

It would be unfair of me to say that it was to my horror that I heard Lestrade offer to show us the alleged scene of the crime and Homes to readily assent. "Good man Lestrade, shall we meet here at ten of the clock upon the morrow?" I realised that I was included in the arrangement when Homes said to me "Watson you could perhaps bring your medical bag, but I doubt if there will be need for you to bring your service revolver!" Lestrade laughed and I attempted a smile. This was typical of Holmes who knew that I was still engaged in medical practice, assuming that this would make no difficulty for me. I muttered that I could get my partner to hold the fort even though I was hardly delighted with the idea of pottering around a house where a horrific murder had taken place with little chance at such a late date of finding anything overlooked by the police and no chance whatsoever of altering that which had been decreed.

To my relief we did at last turn to other topics, including nostalgic reminders of those cases in which we had all three participated. Holmes was for once extremely diplomatic, hardly touching upon Lestrade's doubts and disbeliefs concerning his methods. He said little about that horrific business concerning the multiple murders in the East End, where Lestrade had been far from cooperative, but dwelt more on those cases where his help, through his official status had been invaluable. Such a case had been that in which a horrific hound had terrified several generations of the Baskervilles, both in legend and actuality. It was my turn to be diplomatic in not reminding Holmes of his escapade upon

Dartmoor where he had left me seemingly in charge of the case, only to all but give me a heart seizure with his sudden appearance in the stone age hut!

It was late when Lestrade left us but Holmes, evidently mindless of my own situation was unwilling to consider seeking his bed. Instead he regaled me with stories of his life in Fowlhaven, perhaps sensing that he had given me an overdose of the question of Crippen's innocence or guilt.

Then quite suddenly, as if reading my mind, Holmes turned to face me squarely and said, "My dear fellow I have as even been taking it for granted as to your availability for helping me with my little escapade. I realise that you are still actively practising medicine and may find it difficult to fall in with my plans."

"How did you know that I was still practising, I do not remember saying as much?"

"Oh come, you know my methods Watson. I discerned the iodine stain upon the heel of your right hand. It is still too deep in hue to be more than a day or so old. But even had I missed that detail I believe the frequent consultation you have held with your hunter watch is that of a man whose time is still of value. You will notice that I have lost the habit." He pause, then leaned forward, placing a hand upon my shoulder and said, "Watson, dear old friend, do please humour me upon this one occasion. There may not be much time involved, perhaps only a day or two, so please join me in this, perhaps my last ever investigation." Then he chuckled before saying, "Later you could record it for posterity as *Holmes's Last Case*, although it scarcely counts as a case does it? Anyway, you might get half a dozen pages out of it?"

Chapter Two

Thirty-Nine Hilldrop Crescent

On the following morning I took a taxicab to the Charing Cross Hotel where I found Lestrade and Holmes waiting for me, standing beside a small motor car that Lestrade referred to as a Morris. I was quite startled when I realised that the car belonged to the ex-Inspector because he had been so long retired that I always associated him in my mind with police broughams and hansom cabs. Holmes's mellowness of the previous night had changed to his more usual morning irony that I remembered so well.

"My dear Watson, here you are, bright and early as usual! (It was but ten minutes beyond our agreed meeting time). No doubt your breakfast took longer or perhaps your coffee was too hot to drink at once?"

"I got here as soon as I could Holmes, having had to stop to assist the victim of a road accident." This was true for I had stopped the cab for ten minutes whilst I staunched the blood of a woman who had been injured by a motor car. It was as well that I did because the ambulance was a long time in coming. Then the taxicab driver had insisted on charging me for the time that he had spent in waiting! But I did not mention any of this: at least not my own part in the incident.

"Nice little runner she is Doctor!" Lestrade referred to his little car. "It costs more to run than a horse and trap but it's a lot less trouble, and faster. Leastways, it will be when they get all these wretched horses off the road." I chuckled at this remark, remembering how he had been prone to complain about motor cars in the old days, claiming that they were part of a plot to force down the value of horses!

The machine took rather more than a shake of reins and a walk on command; indeed it took Holmes's strong arm to throw the handle and start the noisy little engine turning. Lestrade beamed as he played around with a contraption which he called a throttle, "Fairly purrs, doesn't she?" I would have called it more of a growl myself. But we sped along at twenty miles an hour at the very least, past the West End and through King's Cross chugging our way along York Way until we reached the Camden Road. A right turn into this road took us to Hilldrop Crescent on our immediate left.

Perhaps not as imposing as those of Nash, Hilldrop Crescent was none the less an impressive semi-circle of some sixty stately residences. Number thirty-nine, although identical in design, proved to be a trifle less well kept in appearance when compared to the rest of the terrace.

Holmes suggested that Lestrade should leave the car in the main road so that we cold make our inspection on foot rather than draw too much attention to our activities. Lestrade decided to leave the Morris beside the church on the corner of Hilldrop Road and Camden Road, and went through a quite extraordinary ritual of locking doors and even removing a small but vital part of the car's mechanism to deter possible car theft. Holmes commended him for his vigilance but gave me a secret facial message that I interpreted as meaning that he doubted if anyone would want to steal that which he obviously regarded secretly as a monstrosity. As if sensing the unspoken Lestrade remarked, "Can't be too careful these days. Only last week a Mercedes was purloined in Liverpool!"

So it was that we strolled as casually as possible back to the fascia of number thirty-nine Hilldrop Crescent, passing it slowly to note from the absence of curtains that it was almost certainly unoccupied, as I for one would have rather expected. There was a housing agency board, planted upon a pole in the front garden. I did not trouble to mention this, for it was too obvious for the other two to miss. But I did mention the slightly shabby exterior. Holmes commented, "The other houses are identically decorated to suggest that there are some kind of regulations; Crippen evidently managed to become the exception to this ruling, probably for financial reasons." I replied with a question, "Could this mean that Crippen knew that he would no longer be here, having already planned his escape to Canada with Ethel le Neve?" Holmes turned to Lestrade. "When did Crippen take up residence here?" Lestrade replied, "In the September of 1905." Holmes said, "The redecoration is more recent than that, so I must agree that your deduction could be valid Watson." Then he spoiled my moment of glory by adding, "Valid, but unlikely!"

Suddenly there was a diversion. I fancied I gained a fleeting glimpse of a figure behind the second floor window. The other two had not noticed it but Holmes took my observation seriously, saying "Come Watson, let us search for the rear of the building whilst Lestrade watches here."

As if by instinct we turned down an alleyway that led through a gap in the terraces, and this took us to an open space at the rear of the buildings. This took the form of a large garden, with a footpath running between it and the backs of the houses, each of which had a tiny yard or garden at its rear. These varied rather in their style for some were brick floored whilst others had neat lawns but all had one thing in common in the exactly similar iron barred gates that had been fitted. These gates and the railings between them appeared to be antique in style, so that despite their smart appearance could well have been fitted when the terrace was built, perhaps a century earlier.

The gardens were deserted save for a lone figure making its way toward us and making for the entrance gate through which we had passed. As the figure grew nearer I perceived it was that of an elderly woman, her body shrouded in black with her head of wild and extremely fair hair and white powdered face making a strange contrast. She pushed a soap box on wheels before her; of the kind usually associated with street urchins and as she came yet nearer we could see that her wild flaxen hair was crowned with a coronet which would have sparkled, had it been recently cleaned, with a great many artificial jewels. As she passed us Holmes touched his cap and I raised my hat, but she turned her head from us and hurried through the gate with the wheels of her soap box squeaking in a horrific manner.

We made no converse concerning this apparition, for there was little to be said concerning such an eccentric derelict, all too common in our big cities more is the pity, but some seconds of silence spoke the compassion which we both felt for the unfortunate soul. We observed no other signs of life save for the rare sight of a fox scurrying across the greensward.

"Unusual to see 'Reynard' in such a built up area Holmes?"

"True Watson, though I will wager he is safer her than in the country, far from the fear of game keepers or red-coated lunatics." (Holmes, as an Englishman, had always had a very rare antipathy toward healthy blood sports).

Despite the absence of numbering at the rear of the terrace we had little difficulty in identifying number thirty-nine through its lack of renewed decoration. I was about to push the iron gate open and enter when Holmes put a restraining hand upon my arm. He chuckled as he said, "Let us inspect the area for spoor before we trample upon it Watson." He stood to one side of the gate and swung it carefully open, inspecting the ground; or rather I should say the path that had its fair share of muddy deposit.

"You see Watson, the old woman has wheeled her contraption both in and out of this gateway."

"I can see tyre tracks certainly and some footmarks. Do you think she could be the apparition from the upper window?"

"Possibly Watson, now let us inspect the back door: you see it is locked, but the lock is of a very simple kind which I could open with my penknife. Oh, do not worry Doctor, I have no intent to do so."

After a further perusal of the rear of the building, through which we noticed the balconies at each floor and an entrance to the basement at the bottom of a short flight of steps, we rejoined Lestrade at the front.

"Anything of interest at the back Mr. Holmes? I have observed no further signs of habitation."

"Very little Lestrade, save for a fox and a derelict woman who seemed to be showing some sign of interest in the rear entrance of number thirty-nine."

The ex-Scotland Yard man looked thoughtful as he said, "We need to take a good look at the inside. However, to gain entrance is beyond my powers. I hardly think that my influence would be of any help."

Holmes spoke very casually as he replied, "Pray do not worry because we can gain entry in a perfectly legal manner by simply asking the letting agent to allow our inspection. We need only show guile in the manner of our true identities. Hardly a very serious deception."

His logic, so basic, had been too obvious for Lestrade or myself. The collapsed agent's board gave us the firm's title, Nicholas Scrooby, Son and Company, at a number in the Holloway Road. We walked down the incline, back to that main thoroughfare by way of the Camden Road. It took only a few minutes, just long enough for us to settle our minds upon each *nom de theatre* which we intended to employ for ourselves! We left the Morris beside the church.

The premises of Nicholas Scrooby, Son and Company proved to be of that musty type beloved of letting agents. The principal piece of furniture was what I believe is usually referred to as a partners desk. Only one half of this was occupied by an elderly man who looked rather more like an undertaker than someone of his calling. Holmes, seemingly quite altered in appearance simply through the donning of a pair of horn rimmed spectacles, played our overture so to speak. "Have I the pleasure of addressing Mr. Scrooby senior or junior?" The doleful gentleman threw up his hands in a

41

gesture of mock sadness, "Both dead Sir, these many years. But my name is Oglethorpe, and I am the company. Whom Sir, might I perhaps have the pleasure to serve?"

Mr Oglethorpe's manner had become changed from one of complete melancholy to one of cringing servitude, quite suddenly, as if to a formula. Holmes responded, "My name is Septimus Hustle and my associates are Messrs. Grimethorpe and Clogg. We are interested in taking a short lease on the property, number thirty-nine Hilldrop Crescent."

At Holmes's words the clerk, the only occupier of the room aside from Oglethorpe and ourselves, made a most spectacular collapse from his high stool. He fell, complete with the ledger that he had been working upon, into a heap upon the floor. It was a fall worthy of one of Sanger's clowns! Oglethorpe made no move to assist the poor fellow so, as a medical man I felt it my duty to go to his aid. I helped him to rise and to regain his perch, returning to him the ledger that he had dropped. He was obviously unhurt, though a little shocked I imagined from his all but gibbering symptoms. Oglethorpe chastised the poor fellow verbally, "Watkins, how can you be so clumsy, pull yourself together, man!"

Actually I had noticed that Holmes's announcement concerning the property which interested him also practically to a point of astonishment which he however seemed to have the presence of mind to attempt to conceal. As it was his manner changed by the second between joy and fear. Joy, I supposed at the thought of the possibility of letting a house with such a bizarre reputation and fear that we would, if ignorant of that reputation, be suddenly be informed of it.

"How did you come to hear about the property and its availability Mr Hustle?"

"Why from your board which lay upon the ground before the house. As this residence was obviously unoccupied I took to thinking that the board alluded to it."

"Quite so, how observant, and how accurate your surmise. Well perhaps you might wish to view the property, in which case I can send Watkins round there with you to open it up and let you see for yourselves what a really desirable residence is involved?"

The closer we got to Hilldrop Crescent during our short return walk the more uneasy Watkins appeared to become. No mention had been made, either by ourselves, or Oglethorpe, regarding the bizarre reputation of the property we were about to inspect, but his manner had been guarded. At length Watkins clearly could not restrain his unease any longer. He said, "I suppose you know all about the trouble at number thirty-nine?" Holmes feigned complete ignorance concerning the property being the scene of the Crippen affair, enquiring, "There has been some sort of trouble at the house we are about to view?"

"Well, yes Sir, you might say there was ... you see, someone died there."

He trailed off with uncertainty in his voice and I spoke to him, taking Holmes's lead of ignorance. "This is not unusual surely is it, in a city where hundreds of people die each day?"

Watkins had lost all sense of duty. Both his hand and his voice shook as he said, "Yes but they don't get poisoned and buried under the floor do they?" Then suddenly his sense of responsibility seemed to return, at least to an extent. He all but gasped, "Mr. Oglethorpe will dismiss me when he hears about what I have said, but even if he does I can't help it. I just cannot enter that house again."

It was Lestrade who enquired, "See a ghost did you?"

Watkins showed some backbone at least when he replied, "You should have been there, to say it was creepy would be a great understatement Sir, you sort of sense a presence, call it a ghost if you will."

I said "Oh come Watkins, you don't believe in ghosts surely?"

He replied, "No, not when I'm safely at home or at the office, but sometimes outdoors at night, when there is very little moonlight, or in a house where you know something eerie has occurred, it's different."

Holmes chastised me with his sharp tongue, "Come, whilst no one can prove the presence of spirits, neither can they be disproved. I never discount that which I cannot explain. Watkins, my friends and I will not disclose to your employer anything that might endanger your position. May I suggest that you take yourself to the nearest café, where you can wait for perhaps half an hour whilst we inspect the property?" As if reading Watkins's thoughts he bestowed half a crown upon him, saying "This is in case you neglected to bring the wherewithal for refreshment with you." Holmes took the key from Watkins, with the promise that we would meet him outside the café in thirty minutes. As he led the way to Hilldrop Crescent he said, "Fate in the form of a nervous underling has given us the time we need to inspect the premises in some sort of privacy."

Watkins's suggestion that number thirty-nine was eerie as far as its interior was concerned proved to be valid from entrance hall to basement and right up to its attic. Of course there is something a little unsettling about empty houses in general, with their bare floorboards and lack of any sort of furnishing. But this particular empty property had an overhanging atmosphere of gloom and sorrow. I realised that this was partially because we knew of the tragedy that had occurred there, but even allowing for this there was something sinister about even the dank smell which seemed to pervade everything and everywhere. Sherlock Holmes sniffed the air eagerly, almost as if he could smell attar of roses! He smiled grimly as he said, "To you Watson, just an unpleasing odour of damp and neglect, but to the trained nose every sniff provides evidence of the history, ancient and modern, of this building, or rather this particular portion of it. I'm sure you are familiar with my monograph upon the subject of the sense of smell as an aid in crime detection. Other senses may be more heavily relied upon, but the sense of smell is just as important. Come let us begin our investigations with the basement where the evidence that led to Crippen's demise was discovered. Time is not upon our side, we have a mere thirty minutes."

I ventured, "Could you not have suggested that Watkins take longer over his refreshment?"

"Watson, more than half an hour would have produced suspicion in both master and servant. Let us be pleased to have the house to ourselves for thirty minutes. Lestrade, may I call upon you to examine the upper part of the building whilst Watson and I survey the basement. We will combine our findings when we get to the ground floor."

We started in the basement, Holmes and I, naturally examining the brick floor of the coal cupboard to find the loose bricks just as we expected. We lifted the bricks to find only the foundations that one would also expect. Holmes examined everything carefully and with an air of disappointment said, "Those clodhopping policeman have left us nothing to speak of."

The basement itself was strangely decorated with pink paint, fairly recently applied. I remarked upon this and its eccentricity to my friend. But Holmes merely remarked, "One winces at the taste of some people Watson, but cannot see of necessity any sinister connection."

We had not the time at this particular point to examine the whole basement in detail, but we made our way shortly to the ground floor and traversed those rooms with interest. There were scars where furniture had stood, and even signs of where carpets had lain, but a passing inspection revealed very little. However, Holmes was intrigued with the signs that floorboards had been recently raised and replaced. "Note Watson that they have been prised up, replaced carefully, but the original screws have been nailed back rather than re-screwed."

"How can you tell on such a casual inspection and without removing as much as a single screw?" He replied, "Notice the residue around each screw Watson, this is a patent compound which is a time saving boon to clumsy carpenters, of which Scotland Yard have their share."

On the upper floor we re-met with Lestrade who told of no particular discovery, save a firmly fixed attic cupboard that presented little opportunity due to its small size and obvious position which could have attracted the attention of the authorities. "The Yard will have been all over that cupboard Mr. Holmes, and I doubt if it held any secrets anyway."

We rejoined Watkins outside the café. We told him that we were interested in taking a short lease on the property. He was relieved that his efforts would be recorded as successful with his employers.

When later we confronted Oglethorpe again, Holmes amazed that individual with an offer for the tenancy of thirty-nine Hilldrop Crescent surely unique in its generosity and brevity. Oglethorpe raised his eyebrows and said, "My dear Mr. Hustle, what must I tell the present owner when he returns from foreign parts to learn that I have let his property for one month only?"

Holmes spoke casually, "You must tell him whatever you wish Sir, also the fact that you gained for him nearly a year's rent for an occupancy of one month only. You know as well as I do that such a notorious address must at this moment in time be all but impossible to sell or rent. But with another tenant to show in your ledgers the situation can only be improved as far as your client is concerned."

Oglethorpe looked thoughtful. The estate agent removed, cleaned and replaced his pince-nez before saying, in perhaps some confusion, "But Sir, I fail to understand the purpose of such a short tenancy and its advantage to yourself?"

In reply Holmes was at his most acidic, saying, "It matters little Mr. Oglethorpe if you understand the situation, just so long as my colleagues and I myself understand it."

After the simple contract had been made and we were enjoying a meal at Simpson's, Lestrade having needed to return to his own domestic activities, Holmes and I discussed the events of the day.

"We have a month to make our investigations Watson, but unfortunately I have first some affairs to attend to in Fowlhaven. Can you manage to stay there for a day or two until my return?"

I believe my reader will have some idea concerning my own lack of enthusiasm for the whole enterprise? But when Sherlock Holmes makes a request he is difficult to refuse ...

"My dear fellow, you are my only friend: there is nobody else I can turn to for help in this matter, where time is important."

"Could Lestrade not help you?"

"A fine sergeant, but a poor adjutant Watson. At this stage I need you to stay at the property, day and night, and observe. Lestrade will liaise with you and keep you supplied with the necessities of life. I ask only for two days and nights of your time, or three at the most and you need to start until tomorrow evening."

The period that he would wish for me to stay at Hilldrop Crescent seemed to be getting longer. I decided that I must strike a bargain with Holmes before the three days and nights became a week.

To an old campaigner like myself the preparation for my seventy-two hour vigil at Holloway presented little difficulty. I needed simply some changes of linen, toiletries, and my camp bed that I had fortunately kept as a souvenir of the Afghanistan campaign. I decided also that I would take my medical bag and service revolver. I trusted Lestrade to play his part in keeping me supplied with comestibles. I understood that there was a water supply to the house that was in operation, but I packed some candles just in case the gas light had been disconnected. A dark lantern completed my equipment for my safari to Hilldrop Crescent.

Holmes handed me the key to the property late the following day. He gave no indication of his progress in the interim as he was in a hurry to return to Fowlhaven. I was undismayed as I journeyed to Holloway. Soon I had unloaded my few articles that would allow me to live in some degree of comfort for the next few days. First I placed the camp bed in a position on the first floor from which I could observe the lawn at the back of the building. My first thought was to examine everything in the house. Naturally I would start with the basement where the murder of Belle Elmore was supposed to have taken place, or rather the place where what few of her remains were discovered. At this point I feel that I should explain to my reader in rather more detail, my feelings

47

concerning Holmes's insistence upon making investigation into the Crippen affair. That I had no great enthusiasm for this campaign of my friends will already have been hinted at. It was only in view of our long friendship that I had allowed myself to become involved in such a seemingly (to me) lost cause. I felt that Crippen had been so clearly guilty of the murder of Belle Elmore that Holmes's discovery of slight inconsistencies was hardly worth following up. Additionally as Crippen had already been condemned and executed the whole exercise appeared to be somewhat pointless. The reader may consider that if an injustice had been done, an admission of this should be made, even if the time to put things right had so long passed.

Of course we also have to consider Lestrade's interest and involvement in the matter. I felt sure that the ex-Detective Inspector from Scotland Yard must have realised that Holmes was following a lost cause. Why then was he allowing himself to become involved? There were several possible answers to this question: his respect for my friend, a genuine desire to promote absolute justice even where a mistake might need to be admitted, or the most likely answer, his boredom with his inactivity in retirement. An old war-horse stamping and snorting at the promise that the game might once more be afoot! So with the doubts that I held concerning the advisability of entering wholeheartedly into Holmes's project I had decided to keep my end of whatever sort of bargain had been struck and hold the fort at Hilldrop Crescent whilst Holmes conducted his essential business in Sussex. But I had determined to inform my friend that I had thereafter my own affairs to conduct, which was indeed true. My decision to examine the property from basement to attic whilst I was on the premises was merely to pass the time.

In the basement I examined the loose floor bricks that had figured so much in the evidence at Crippen's trial. Of course there was little left to find save brick dust and similar compounds. All forensic evidence had long ceased to be available, either to the naked eye or to my lens: though had Holmes been present it is possible that he might have spotted something that I had missed. A cursory examination of the entire basement revealed nothing to me, save that the pink wall paint appeared to have been fairly recently applied; possibly at Crippen's instigation when he had taken up residence in the building. We knew that he and his wife had occupied the basement and had let rooms to various other tenants in the rest of the house.

The ground floor in its turn seemed to reveal little that was significant. The rear window gave a good view of the back lawn and the balcony an even better one. I looked for anything that might help an investigation of the kind that Holmes was undertaking, but of course it was difficult to know just what to look for that could help a lost cause!

The second floor appeared equally barren of answers to any questions that I might ask through observation or investigation. There remained only the attic to be tackled. Fortunately there was a ladder, obviously stationed in the otherwise empty room especially to provide access to the topmost area. I took a battery lantern with me as I climbed up to investigate the attic of number thirty-nine Hilldrop Crescent.

Chapter Three

A Grisly Surprise

When I reached the top of the ladder and pushed up the panel which needed to be moved to give access to the attic I suppose upon reflection I expected to find another empty apartment, bereft of anything to stimulate my interest. At first it seemed as if this were so, but after a careful inspection I found a panel in a sloping wall which appeared to be of rather more recent origin than its surrounding surfaces. Like its fellows the panel was secured by undisguised screws, but like the wood itself the screwheads looked recent. As far as I could see there was little sign of rust or pitting. I determined to loosen them that I might remove them to see if anything lay beyond. In order to do this I needed a tool that might fit the slots of the screwheads. I descended the ladder to see if anything I had brought with me would serve the purpose. I had not brought any actual tools but turned at once to the bag of forks and cutlery. There was not a blade among them that was square enough at its pointed end to be of any use. Returning to the attic I was reduced to experimenting with my pocket knife. Had I wanted to pull a cork, bore a hole or even remove a stone from a horse's hoof I would have been able to manage after a fashion.

There were two blades, one smaller than the other. I tried to insert the smaller blade into one of the slots. The blade tended to fold back towards the body of the knife.

Every time the tip of the blade slipped out of the slot, which was frequent during my inept attempt at carpentry. Then a fortunate accident restored my confidence. The blade slipped again, but this time its pointed tip snapped cleanly, leaving me holding that which looked for all the world like a screwdriver. It was not easy to use as such due to its tendency to close, but by careful handling and concentration I was able to loosen the screws.

When I had lifted the panel out and peered inside the aperture that I had created by the light of my lantern I uttered aloud my reaction of bewilderment and horror. For there lay a partly open sack which revealed a pile of bones. Were they human? Possibly, but I knew that close examination would be required to make this certain. Were they recent or had they been laying hidden for a long while? They looked aged, but again examination would be necessary to provide a definite answer.

Remembering that there was a large flat built in shelf in the central first floor room I bundled the sack down to that apartment that I might spread the bones flat and examine them. Luckily, as I had already discovered, the gas light was still connected which made this easier even in an otherwise dark corner. Moreover I had the battery lamp as an additional form of illumination. I quickly surmised that the bones were human, and not all those of the same human being. A high percentage were almost certainly those of a male person, discernible from their size and style. But a lesser number were clearly female. No skulls were among my find, but there were ribs aplenty, loose and damaged, likewise forearms, thigh bones and smaller ones that had once been those of hands and feet. All exhibited the stain of age and appeared to have been gouged, as flesh had been removed from them, probably with a cleaver, for many of the bones were fractured, as if roughly handled by a butcher! From their colouration I estimated that they could have been several years in the attic.

I realise that the reader may find my description a little cold blooded, so I will explain at this point that even a hardened medical man of science finds the handling of such remains far from pleasant. However, when you have been an army medic one is able to face these situations without despair or abhorrence. Also within a short while one's factual curiosity replaces other reactions. I was intrigued by the fact that someone had hacked human flesh from the bones, and yet left no sign of so much as a tiny scrap or residue adhering to them. Almost as if they had been boiled.

This examination of my gruesome discovery took some hours. Then, the sorting of the bones took time also, with the eventual placing into specimen bags (which I had had the foresight to bring with me) of those bones and fragments that I believed might have belonged to an individual body. Afterwards as the daylight started to fade I started the task of making as full a documentation of my find in a note book. As I sat with pen and ink at my travelling writing desk I was interrupted by a blinding flash of a rather unusual kind. The weather had been far from thundery and I doubted that it was part of a sudden storm. Being alone in that place of such grisly reputation and having so recently tackled such a grisly task my imagination, at least for a few seconds fairly run away with me. I am not given to being over imaginative, yet I could not stop my memory from reminding me of that glimpse of a figure at the window of this house, assumed by us all to be empty.

After my first transfixation at this strange flash of light I peered out of the back window onto the communal lawn. There in the twilight I could make out the figure of an elderly man with a mane of white hair who appeared to be preoccupied by a huge camera upon a tripod. He dived under his black photographer's cloth with his right arm extended, holding a T shaped contraption from which another, even more terrifying flash emitted. So that was the answer to the seeming ghostly illumination, a photographer's flash powder?

I emerged from the back door and wandered onto the lawn to confront this rather eccentric looking person. As I walked towards the camera there was yet another blinding flash, but it did not seem to come from the same source as before.

Rather it seemed to emit from the roof of a small shed that appeared to have a small camera built onto its roof.

"I'm sorry, I thought you were someone else!" The voice rang out across the lawn. I replied, "Who were you expecting?" The reply was very strange, "No one earthly Sir, I was expecting someone of another plane!"

I was somewhat taken aback but continued as best I could, "My colleagues and I are staying at number thirty-nine for a short while to conduct some research. We are interested in urban wildlife ... (I was desperate) ... for example the foxes that have found their way here from the heath."

He replied, "Foxes, badgers, quite a few of our dear fellow creatures. But I am more interested in the occult Sir, I photograph those who have passed on. I am especially interested in the gentleman who occupied the very house where you now reside, namely Dr. Crippen, who I feel sure must traverse this particular area since his execution."

I was not merely surprised by his words, rather I was shocked. But I had a mental picture of Sherlock Holmes wagging a long slim finger prior to saying, 'Even if you do not believe Watson, do not discount!' None the less I have always had difficulty in affecting seriously the expounded theories of the stark raving mad! How could this seemingly sane, even learned man seriously suggest that he might expect a visit from Crippen's ghost?

I tried not to betray my own rather one sided views concerning the supernatural by asking, "Why do you suppose that he would wish to revisit these, to him, unhappy scenes?" He considered, "Oh, for a number of reasons probably, though I can only really be sure concerning one. He seeks justice Sir, justice!"

Maybe I felt a certain relief that there was another person other than Sherlock Holmes who believed in a possibility concerning the innocence of Crippen, even though that person might be one that I suspected of being a lunatic! I asked him, "What leads you to suspect an injustice?" He replied, "Because he was not an unintelligent man Sir; indeed he was a confidence trickster on a considerable scale and on two continents. He would have been too smart to make that clumsy and obvious attempt to escape by sea, with his lady disguised as a boy. He knew that the pair of them would be discovered and apprehended; though I don't imagine she did or she would hardly have been party to the enterprise. She must have imagined that he had an added escape plan up his sleeve."

I said, "She was exonerated from involvement in the murder." He replied, "Quite rightly so, but then neither did Crippen have any involvement."

At this point I was about to leave and return to thirty-nine Hilldrop Crescent when he said, "Come into my darkroom Sir, and I will show you some interesting pictures that I have taken." I was tempted to refuse his invitation, but I thought that Holmes would have wished me to pursue the situation. He opened the impressive little outbuilding with a key to open the padlock that held it secure.

Inside he lit the interior with a red photographic bulb that illuminated everything in a rather eerie fashion. There were all the usual dishes and tanks of chemicals that one would expect in the photographer's darkroom. But that which he showed me was of particular interest, being some plates and portions of film connected with the comings and goings of various personages. These were dated and of significant interest. There was one of the derelict woman whom Holmes and I had encountered, and one of a particularly unpleasant looking individual, dirty, bearded and shabby.

At this moment I realised that I had not introduced myself so I said, "My name is Grimethorpe, John Grimethorpe." He clasped my hand and said, "Montmorency, Major George Montmorency, at your service Sir." We shook hands and I realised that I must carry on as if I considered him to be perfectly normal.

I decided that the time had come for me to return to the house and I did so not without a certain melancholy, for its atmosphere was not one that made me rejoice in the fact that I must sleep there, alone. Although I am an old soldier, and a man of science and not given to being over imaginative, the atmosphere of the late Dr. Crippen's house was hardly one of the jollity nor yet of tranquillity. I turned and bid my new acquaintance good evening. As a passing shot he said, "Watch out for Crippen's shade. They are usually harmless but in his case who can say?" I hurried away lest he should think of any additional remarks of comfort!

Not wishing at this point to experiment with the aged gas cooker where doubtless Belle Elmore had raised many a midnight snack upon her return from the theatre, I fitted together the long neglected spirit heater of my campaigning days. I was about to bring forth the sausages that I had fortunately remembered to bring, only to find that I had forgotten to bring some spirit for the stove. I admit that under my breath I muttered a few words that had not escaped my lips since those days in Afghanistan! However, I looked on the bright side. This meant that I must seek nourishment from without the house, and this thought was a relief rather than an annoyance. Darkness had descended and I looked forward to an expedition through the brightly lit north London streets. Of course I realised that it had been Holmes's plan that I should not leave the immediate vicinity save in an emergency, but then the ravages of hunger seemed to represent such a situation. Thus having salved my conscience I set forth.

Once I had left thirty-nine Hilldrop Crescent I became more optimistic, and I reckoned that a hot meal would complete this becalming process. Of course I had thus far only seen the area that surrounded me by day, and all districts tend to appear quite different by night. The bright street lights had not yet given way to the modern electric lamps. I had in my mind the picture of the lamplighter, at this very moment lighting the final lamp in the Camden Road. This in its turn led me to dwell upon Robert Louis Stevenson's beautiful little poem *The Lamplighter* and to complete the thought circle I was saddened by the memory of Stevenson's death from consumption at such an early age. In the days of which I write this disease was a scourge, caused by damp living conditions and undernourishment. Then as if by means of some theatrical cue I noticed a large number of derelicts, among them the very same menacing looking fellow who had been caught upon my new eccentric friend's camera.

As I passed the large church on the corner of Hilldrop Road and Camden Road I noticed to my surprise that a large number of derelicts were gathered outside its doors as if waiting for the huge oaken entrance wings to be cast open. Most of them looked, to be perfectly frank, more in need of material than spiritual aid. I also noticed that the church had no announcements or list of services outside of it, not yet even a title board.

From here I spied a small shop that as it transpired was still open and stocked the spirit I needed for my stove. I next settled upon a small café that was situated a mere two hundred yards or so down the hill from the aforementioned church. It was the kind of eating establishment which I would not usually frequent, but the pangs of hunger were fast gathering and the Holloway Road with its more suitable places seemed at that moment to be a long way off. I entered the not very prepossessing entrance and sat at a table assuming that sooner or later a waiter or waitress would arrive to see to my requirements. But it turned out to be later rather than sooner. I glanced around to find that the other patrons appeared to have been attended to. Then the female vagrant (she of the photograph and earlier encounter) walked in, placing her wheeled cart just inside the café doors. She glanced round, her glittering tiara tilting dangerously. She could see that the table I occupied had the only spare seat. She occupied it and after noisily blowing her nose on her scarf spoke.

"Ee won't letcha sit there unless you buys something." She evidently assumed that the empty space upon the marble tabletop was due to my unwillingness to purchase comestibles. I tried to explain, "The waiter has not yet appeared." She looked at me through eyes that looked like currents set in a vast kneaded ball of dough and said, "No and not likely to 'cause there ain't no waiter. You 'as to fetch it yerself love!"

I had never patronised a café that did not employ someone to wait at table before. I walked up to the counter behind which stood a vast man with a fork in one hand and several sausages in the other. He looked at me unkindly over steel rimmed glasses and made an enquiry which sounded like 'Yerstz?' To this I enquired, "May I please have some sausages, a fried egg, fried bread and perhaps some fried potato?"

There was a terrifying silence quite suddenly, and all eyes were upon me. After what seemed like an hour but was yet a few seconds the vast man spoke to me. He said, "Can't hear you!" Thinking him to be hard of hearing I repeated my order with a far louder tone. He still shook his head and continued to look at me unkindly. I did not shout my order because I realised that deafness was not the problem The derelict woman came to my aid again, shambling over to me and pulling my sleeve and muttering, "Top of the bill Bertie love, just ask for the top of the bill Bertie." Bewildered I did as she had bid me to. This time he nodded his head and all was serene until I added, "And a cup of coffee?" The old woman shook her head sadly and prompted me again, "Ask him for a fourpenny one."

A few minutes later with the meal and coffee before me I asked the woman to explain why I needed to order my food and drink in what seemed to me like a foreign language. She explained "Well it's like a sort of code love, all the fry-ups are called top of the bill, but Bertie is the one that 'cludes everything. Now Billy ain't got no fried potato. Charlie 'as no fried bread either and so on."

"Why is a cup of coffee called a fourpenny one?"

"Oh 'cause it costs fourpence; I say, you're a bit slow!"

I told her that I understood, but could not see a reason for having to order food by cypher! However, she told me that it kept strangers away. I had always believed that the whole idea of running a café was to serve food to as many people as possible and practical. But then I told myself that it must be some kind of kitchen of thieves where the patrons did not wish to be overheard by strangers. But I left it at that, for the food was very satisfying, excellent value, and also I thought I might learn more from the old woman that would be of interest to myself and Sherlock Holmes. This proved to be so. She said, "The Doctor tried to worm his way in here, but he was never really 'cepted. We all thought 'ee was a bit dodgy. Belle now, she was different ..."

My heart all but missed a beat as unprompted by me she had started to talk about Crippen and Belle Elmore. "She was my friend, a lovely woman, even gave me this tiara. I used to go round there and visit her when he was at his workplace. She and I would crack a bottle of the old mother's ruin. I saw her last just a few weeks before I heard about her murder. I didn't go after that because she told me she was going away, taking a trip. Said she had sold all her jewels except the tiara, which she gave me. They said in the papers that he had pawned 'em, but you see he didn't know about most of them. She was ill poor love, a little too much gin for too many years. Said she was going away, but she didn't know then that she was going forever. That beast, I danced in the street the day they 'anged him!" She wept and I tried to comfort her, first with words and then with a half sovereign. This latter tactic worked splendidly. Her tears disappeared and her eyes sparked as she said, "Won't need to go to the church tonight. I can go to the Nags Head for 'alf quarten of gin and a bit of grub. I'm sick of his old pies anyway, and he ain't a proper vicar anyway."

I can assure my reader that a little more bribery soon provided me with the lurid story of an unfrocked vicar who had taken a lease on the old church at the corner of Hilldrop Road and turned it into a sort of unofficial soup kitchen, and where he provided shelter each night for the homeless without demanding that they sing hymns or say their prayers. To all this she added, "Chucked out the church for being too fond of the ladies he was, and by the way he lived at thirty-nine Hilldrop Crescent before the Crippens moved in."

At this I fairly started: I had calmly accepted the unfrocked vicar dispensing food and shelter to the homeless, and the information concerning some of the last movements of Belle

Elmore, but these ceased to be wonders falling into my lap compared to the coincidence of the house that had sheltered Crippen having been the earlier residence of the vicar. (I use that simple title because in my bewilderment I had forgotten to ask the homeless woman the cleric's name).

The inner man provided for and some possibly valuable information gained I felt so much better as I strolled back up the Camden Road. Upon reaching the church on the corner I noticed that the doors were open wide and the crowd of vagrants were not to be seen. I was curious to know if they were within and so I quietly edged around one of the doors. I was accosted by a tall dark suited man. He smiled at me with teeth that were just a little bit large for his mouth. He was middle aged and with not too much dark hair, greying at the temples. I determined to take in as much detail as possible that I might convey this to Holmes. I remembered also that I needed his name. He spoke first, "Good evening Sir, my name is Slade, Frederick Slade, whom may I have the pleasure of addressing?" I replied, "My name Sir, is John Hustle. I did not intend to intrude upon your scene. I, well, to be honest, I was frankly curious."

From the corner of my eye I could see a mass of unkempt beings and could hear their upraised voices: some of them singing, others shouting and yet others indulging in what could only be described as drunken chanting. The ex-vicar, Mr. Slade put an arm around my shoulder and led me gently but firmly away from the church entrance. When we reached the pavement he said, "Forgive me Sir, but I prefer my poor unfortunate friends to be well prepared before we receive visitors. You see they are not as fortunate as you or I. Often I think of them as my wayward children for although all adult many have minds like those of a child. Others have problems with the demon drink and things even worse. (He cast an upward glance of sorrow). I take them in so that they will not die upon the streets and feed them, asking no questions in return or trying to make them sing hymns or chant in return. I believe that in the decade that I have operated thus I have gained some ground, for each year I seem to be dealing with fewer such unfortunates. You may give a donation if you wish, towards the soup and pies which I provide.'

I fumbled in my pockets and produced a sovereign. This evidently pleased him and he shook me warmly by the hand asking, "Do you reside in this area Mr. Hustle?" I replied, "Why yes, quite near." He said, "Capital, so the next time we meet I can introduce you to my flock, having given them ample warning of your coming. You see, they have their pride Mr. Hustle, they have their pride."

Slade and I parted on seemingly affable terms, yet I felt his slight resentment of my intrusion, despite my donation to his cause. I returned to the house with a feeling that I had made a good start with my own contribution to what I had almost come to think of as Holmes's lost cause. Perhaps there was some point in his investigating the Crippen case after all.

Chapter Four

My Report

My first night spent at thirty-nine Hilldrop Crescent was hardly the most peaceful or comfortable that I have ever spent. I had decided to retire at a later hour, namely two o'clock in the morning, in order that I would be too tired to be of over imaginative mind. It had been rather an eventful day, with incidents and discoveries, some bizarre, some quite sinister but all thought provoking when viewed dispassionately.

It must have been at three o'clock when the first interruption occurred. I had just about started to doze off when suddenly there was an unholy screaming and shouting that rent the until then peaceful night. It worried me for some half a minute until I realised that it was coming from the direction of the church. It was a mild and dry night: perhaps the shelterers had decided to leave the church. However, the noise abated and I tried once more to sleep. Alas this simple natural function, although not much to ask for was, I finally decided, to be denied to me. I arose, partly I dressed and I lit the spirit stove to make a pot of tea. I whistled bright military marches to hold up my spirits and even strode up and down in time with these refrains. As I swallowed a few mouthfuls of the comfortingly strong tea I mused upon how to spend the rest of the hours of darkness with some sort of profit to be gained from them. If I could not sleep I must at least work.

Eventually I decided to compose a report for Sherlock Holmes upon my adventures and findings of the day that had just passed. However important his home emergencies I knew he would be anxious for information. I will give the reader some idea as to the style of this document. It is not entirely accurate because I never again saw it, let alone kept it as reference for the final relation of the story that I tell, but my memory usually serves me well.

FIRST REPORT TO SHERLOCK HOLMES

39 Hilldrop Crescent,
Early Wednesday morning.

My Dear Holmes,

I list the following facts and events in chronological order rather than that of importance, but even so I believe the first discovery rather to be head and shoulders above the others.

1. After first settling into the house I made a thorough search for anything of importance that you may have missed. In the attic, having discovered a panel that had obviously been fairly recently disturbed I opened this, not without difficulty to discover human remains in the shape of a collection of bones. They were clearly not entirely from the same skeleton as some are male and some are female. From their condition the bones have been lying in their hiding place for many months if not even a few years. They are darkened and damaged as if the flesh had been gouged from them with a knife, but not by a practised surgeon. Indeed this scarring is pronounced enough to suggest that they could have been gnawed by some creature. Only proper scientific study in a laboratory can reveal more than this at present.

---

2. Almost immediately following this discovery and examination I discovered a rather eccentric ex-military person, a Major George Montmorency upon the communal lawn at the rear of the building. He had disturbed me by the use of flashlights of the photographic variety. He admitted to me that he was trying to photograph the ghost or shade of Dr. Crippen! I followed the example that you have so often impressed upon me, not to discount anything. The Major took me into a shed where he showed me plates and finished photographic prints which showed that he had secretly taken pictures of that strange homeless woman we encountered earlier and a surly, ill-kempt looking fellow of the kind that I would not wish to meet on a dark night. Evidently he is able to take these pictures using a system whereby the subject triggers both lens and flashlight through treading upon a certain area of the ground.

3. Passing the church upon the corner of Hilldrop Road I pondered upon the fact that it has no identification or church notices at its entrance. Moreover a crowd, evidently waiting for the doors to be opened did not exactly suggest the average body of worshippers. However, I will enlarge upon this in proper order.

4. Needing to support 'the inner man' I attempted to patronise an eating establishment and discovered a very strange one quite close to home. Having overcome a minor difficulty requiring the breaking of a code I encountered the homeless woman. Through a combination of bribery and acumen I discovered that she had been friendly with the late Belle Elmore, who in fact had given her the tiara that we had earlier noticed. From her I learned that she had known both Crippen

and Bell Elmore. She obviously had disliked him and had got on well with his wife with whom she had frequently shared a bottle of gin. A short time before the discovery of the crime Belle had told her that she was going away and so her visits had ceased. Then she told me of an unfrocked vicar who was running a sort of soup kitchen at the church that I have mentioned. I later met the vicar of dubious past, a Mr. Slade. He made it clear that he did not wish me to pry upon his charity work in the church. Of course Holmes all of this pales into insignificance I know when compared with my discovery of the grisly remains at 39 Hilldrop Crescent, and I must admit that it was that discovery which made me determined to continue with something which I had felt to be rather a lost cause. However, I now have the feeling that there is so much more to the Crippen case than has been found by the authorities. Rely upon my co-operation.

I await your instructions,

Your sincere friend,

John H. Watson

In presenting the reader with this version of my report I may perhaps be accused of offering the same facts to him as already related. However, I determined to do so for the sake of completeness, and because I thought it would interest the reader to see just how much of that which I had learned was considered by myself worth the while to convey to my friend. It will doubtless intrigue the reader to ponder upon just why I had omitted certain data.

I sealed my report in a foolscap envelope and having addressed it to Holmes at Fowlhaven, stamped it in readiness to drop into the pillar box later that day.

After one sleepless night and much activity I was able to sleep by five o'clock, uninterrupted and dreamless until seven o'clock. I then arose and had washed, shaved and made myself some coffee by the time Lestrade arrived.

"Good morning Doctor, I trust you slept well?" Lestrade sounded genuinely concerned for my well-being. He sat on my spare camp chair and sipped at the coffee that I had poured him. I told him that I had indeed slept well, but that this was only through exhaustion. I told him that I had written a report for Holmes that he kindly offered to post for me. Then he handed me a large manila envelope inside which he explained that I would find some press reports, published around the time of Crippen's trial that he thought I might find to be of interest. I thanked him and told him just a little concerning my adventures of the previous day, though going into very little detail and omitting altogether my discovery of the bones, thinking that Holmes would want to hear of certain things before anyone else. The ex-Inspector then handed me a small, strung grocery carrier saying, "A few eggs, some bacon and a few other odds and ends in case you don't get an opportunity to go shopping Dr. Watson."

I was indeed grateful for Lestrade's thoughtful ministrations and begged him to keep in touch with me, which he promised to do. Then, taking my report, destined for Sherlock Holmes, he departed. I was happy in the knowledge that this would catch a post early enough for it to reach Fowlhaven upon the morrow. I anticipated that Holmes would himself appear upon the day following that, and would at least have something to ponder upon during his train journey.

Taking the press reports I spread them upon my camp bed and reclined there in comfort to peruse them. They varied between the purely trivial sensationalism and just one or two that captured my interest. Those from the yellow press all had one thing in common; they dismissed Belle Elmore as being less than talented in her profession as a variety artiste. But a couple of the clippings, one in particular, suggested otherwise. This was headlined 'The Belle Elmore I Knew' and was in the form of an interview between 'our crime reporter' and a Mr. Clarkson Rose, described as that well known comedy entertainer and pantomime dame. I feel sure that the following excerpt from the interview will intrigue the reader as it did me ...

During the act of transforming himself from the lady from Kensington back into his normal male self, Mr. Rose said, "I suppose newspaper readers must find it more interesting or sensational if poor old Belle is described as third rate or unsuccessful as a performer. Why otherwise would they describe a quite accomplished soubrette and singer in those terms. She may not have been a second Marie Lloyd, but she was worthy of a place upon any variety bill. She was also a very useful artiste in a concert party or pantomime. Several times she played Aladdin to my Widow Twankey. Latterly she was locked into an unhappy marriage as I need hardly tell you. This caused her to drink a little bit too much, which made her rather unreliable. Without Crippen she would have been fine."

There were a couple of other comments among the clippings in interviews with other stage artistes which took much the same path. But the greater number of the press stories appeared to have fallen into that trap as suggested by Mr. Rose, inasmuch as they referred to her as second rate, fading artiste or fallen star. Alas, I mused, I would never have the chance to judge this for myself, but vowed that I would try and contact Mr. Clarkson Rose. Obviously he had known Belle Elmore well enough to perhaps shine more light upon the subject of her demise and its circumstances.

With these thoughts in mind I decided to go in search of a theatrical newspaper of the kind that might give me some idea where I might contact Clarkson Rose. At the nearest newsagents I was able to obtain a copy of *The Era*, a journal that I remembered from a previous case in which Sherlock Holmes and I had been connected. I suffered the usual banter from the girl behind the counter that one would expect. I realised that my appearance was somewhat less than theatrical. She demanded to know of my particular talent and I told her that I was a siffleur, hoping that she would not know the meaning of the word. Unfortunately she did, saying, "Our delivery boy is one of those too. Whistles *The Jolly Brothers* just as good as Albert Whelan!"

My return to the house in Hilldrop Crescent was uneventful, but little did I know what a startling event would await me there.

I stood transfixed as I glanced up at the front window of my temporary abode. There, seemingly unafraid of being perceived I saw the vagrant man of the photograph captured by the automatic arrangement of the Major! The fellow saw me and evidently knew of my residence, yet made no attempt to hide from my view. Patting my jacket to reassure myself that I had not forgotten to carry my service revolver I made for the back of the building, planning to enter through the basement door. I did this that I might possibly gain time and surprise him by the direction from which I appeared at our confrontation. My thoughts raced as I did this, trying to fathom some possible explanation other than breaking and entering. He had showed no fear at my approach, so perhaps Lestrade had brought him there and was with him?

Managing everything as stealthily as possible I made my way up to the first floor, throwing the door open and revolver in hand confronting the rascal who appeared to be alone in the house. "Who are you and what do you think you are doing here?" I made my voice as authoritative as I could in a tone that would hardly have shamed Stentor of old!

"Keep your 'air on old covey, I ain't doin' no 'arm!" The fellow amazed me with his audacity as I said, "No harm ...

you break into my house and tell me that you are doing no harm? As a matter of interest how did you gain entry?" He snorted before saying, "With a key o' course. The Doctor give it me."

My mind dwelt for a moment on the fact that if this uncouth and possibly dangerous fellow had a key he could have murdered me in my sleep, such as it had been, But I did not pursue that particular point being too interested in the possibility of 'the doctor' being who I thought he might have been. I all but snapped my question, "You mean Crippen?" He was a long time answering and I had some seconds to survey his unkempt, unshorn features and his disgusting attire that would have made any navvy or dustman look almost elegant by comparison. Eventually he said, "Yus, Dr. Crippen ... oh my gosh ..." At this point I thought he was on the verge of an asthmatic spasm. His wheezing cough, however, turned into loud laughter. I shouted at him, "Pull yourself together Sir, explain yourself!"

Suddenly the fellow spoke to me in far from uncultured tones, "Oh, my dear fellow, you are without doubt the most endearingly unsuspecting investigator ever, at least where disguise is concerned. Is this the fourth, or maybe even fifth, time that I have deceived you in this manner? Pray put that revolver away, you are making me quite nervous with it."

As it quickly occurred to my mind that I was addressing Sherlock Holmes in an extremely effective impersonation of a vagrant I decided to say little until I had calmed myself. On some of those previous occasions to which he had referred I had remonstrated with him. This time, instead I quietly replaced my service revolver inside my jacket and watched silently as he sat in one of my camp chairs and brought forth from the depths of his tatters a pipe of the kind that he would normally smoke, casting aside the broken clay that was part of his impersonation. I sat also and gazed, bemused as he filled the pipe from my very own supply of tobacco that he had quickly found among my camping accoutrements. At long last I could trust myself to speak. "The disguise is a good one, for you exactly resemble the fellow that the Major out on the lawn captured with his camera."

"Of course I do Watson, for it was I whom he captured with his lens and shutter."

"Then you must have been in this vicinity rather than attending to matters on the coast?"

"Correct Watson, I have never been far away from you."

"So I sent you a report that was a complete waste of time. Worse, you have never even seen it!"

"*Au contraire* Watson, I studied it with interest. You gave it to Lestrade to post but of course he handed it to me."

"Oh, so you took Lestrade into your confidence but not myself who you have long declared to be your closest, nay only friend? Well this is hardly surprising given the example of your lack of trust. Or did you deceive just to play some boyish prank? If so you really should begin to act your age Holmes!"

Sherlock Holmes looked at me with what I assumed to be a kindly expression. (It was difficult to judge this, given his disguise.) He said, "Come Watson, you must admit that you were upon the brink of telling me that your own affairs would prevent you from assisting me in my present activity; which, you must admit that you considered to be somewhat pointless? My harmless deception has been justified in my retention of your invaluable services."

I grunted and replied, "But if you were going to stay in the vicinity yourself what possible purpose could my presence here have served?'

His reply was immediate and sincere in tone, "My dear fellow, there is no guarantee that I would have gleaned the valuable information that you cunningly extracted from the Major, and the poor creature with the tiara, not to mention the matter of the unfrocked parson, but more of him anon. Oh, and I am forgetting the matter of your discovery of the bones: this was your *piece de resistance*; I am amazed that you have not by now spread them before me!"

Did I detect a tiny touch of sarcasm in his voice? I could not be sure and gave my friend the benefit of the doubt. I fetched the sack of bizarre remains and spread them before him just as he had expected me to have done. Holmes's production of a pipe from amidst his pathetic rags had mildly surprised me but when he materialised a lens from the same source I was quite taken aback. He surveyed the bones carefully, as I had done myself. Then after what seemed an age he said, "Were we at Fowlhaven I could examine them using the scientific equipment which I have there and could make a more pronounced judgement. However, I can see that the bones are a mixed bag of male and female remains and were perhaps in the place where you found them for several years if not longer, judging by their staining. The flesh appears to have been hacked from them with a fairly sharp implement. But then Watson you have yourself discovered these simple facts beyond which neither of us can proceed without equipment and chemicals."

I said, "Yes Holmes, but you can surely hazard some opinions concerning their actual presence here. Some of these bones may be part of the body of Belle Elmore that was never found. But are we dealing with evidence indicating that far from being innocent, Crippen was in fact a double murderer?"

But to my surprise Holmes seemed to be losing interest in my (I had believed) incredible discovery, saying, "Come Watson, we cannot dwell productively upon the bones until we have the services of a pathologist. Let us therefore follow upon other discoveries that we have made." These words, I must be honest with the reader, were quite hurtful to me. But then I suppose my expectation of enthusiasm by Holmes had made me expect too much.

Trying to change the subject, perhaps a little too heartily, I questioned Holmes concerning certain activities of his own. I enquired, "Holmes, where have you been sleeping; surely you do not return to the Charing Cross Hotel at night in your present get up and expect to be admitted?" He chuckled, "No Watson, I have been allowed to sleep in the unnamed church upon the corner by the disgraced cleric. This had fitted in well with my plans, and my impersonation is enhanced by such an environment, and the other sad cases are inclined to share secrets when the cheap gin has loosened their tongues." Perhaps a little bemused when presented with these facts, I asked, "Shall you be returning to the church tonight?" He answered in the affirmative then saying, "Why do we not go to the café where the menu is in code?" I'm surprised that we did not run into each other yesterday. Really it is excellent value Watson, being honest provender of the kind required by a man living on the streets."

Our entrance into the café was quite spectacular for though I had tried to dress as casually as the limited clothing that I had brought with me would allow, there was yet some considerable contrast between us! The other customers surveyed us with curiosity and I felt it would seem least surprising if I purchased the meal for Holmes as well as my own, as if I were some sort of generous philanthropist. The terse café owner eyed me with a sort of grudging approval as I displayed my knowledge of his code; "Top of the bill Bertie, a fourpenny one and a wad and double it!" We were both soon tucking into a meal that would have caused Mrs. Hudson to swoon in horror.

I was quite surprised at how heartily Holmes tackled the fare, bearing in mind his somewhat aesthetic selection of food. As ever he all but read my mind, saying, "Yes Watson, but it is the best of the fare upon offer, beside which it creates a better impression that I appear to be hungry."

After some silence during which Holmes finished his plate of fare he continued.

"Ah, so the old woman's glittering headpiece was genuine after all." I followed my friend's gaze in order to try and follow the words he uttered and I soon spotted the glittering tiara hanging from a nail behind the counter. I had to agree that it certainly it did appear to be the tiara in question but failed to see how he could confirm the validity of the stones, especially at such a distance if he had been unable to do so when we had seen her at closer quarters. "Until this minute I had only seen the article upon the lady's head and rather obscured by strands of hair. You see Watson, it is the clear sight of the setting rather than the stones themselves that tell the story. Even from this distance I can see a quality in the mount which would never have been used as a setting for paste."

At Holmes's request I asked the café owner concerning the tiara before we left. He said, "Reckon poor old Maude 'ad a haccident. Her tirara was found in the grass back of them big houses; the ones where old Crippen lived. It stays on that there nail until either she comes in and spots it, or else until I knows for sure what has happened to her."

Upon leaving the cafe we discussed what the owner had said and we agreed that he was behaving in a very responsible manner, considering that a valuable article was involved. Then as we continued to mount the hill I started to discuss our future plans. I asked, "Do you still intend to continue your habitation at the church Holmes?" His reply was rather as I expected it to be, "For the time being Watson, and I know you have plenty to occupy your time. There is your quest for Mr. Clarkson Rose for example. Oh, come my dear fellow, I did send you some newspaper clippings by way of Lestrade."

I said, "There were a number of them, so how could you know which of them I planned to follow up on?"

My friend chuckled, "Only one of them was of a directly theatrical nature, and I have observed the copy of *The Era* each time you unbuttoned your jacket."

Before going to follow our designated paths we decided to combine in a search of the lawns at the rear of the house. However, with the somewhat bizarre differences in our characterisations we thought it wise to make separate forays and to afterwards compare impressions. It was decided that I should make the first expedition and so I strode forth to see what I could discover. I followed the trail that I would have expected old Maude to make, watching especially for wheel tracks that could have been made by her cart They were not hard to find, although I had to be sure not to confuse old tracks for fresh ones. There had be been little or no rain, so this was not too difficult, the damp turned earth being clear where the fresh tracks stood out. As I followed this spoor I suddenly found an irregular tyre mark, as if the cart had perhaps been tipped or turned.

I soon discovered what had caused Maude to have some sort of a mishap with her cart. There was a somewhat uneven patch of mud. Taking out my penknife I found just beneath the muddy surface a pressure pad, which I guessed must have been the motivation for one of the Major's camera releases. Replacing the mud as carefully as possible I moved along towards the huts. Suddenly the Major appeared as if from nowhere. "Good afternoon Sir, out for a constitutional?"

His words held an acid touch which made me realise that my only sensible move was to take a chance and put my cards on the table; moreover he could see that I was, or had been, monkeying with his shutter release equipment. I replied, "No Major, I nearly fell over your hidden camera release. I was out here looking to see if I could find any sign of the poor old lady who lives rough, for I have heard that she seems to have been missing from her usual haunts. I suppose you haven't seen her?"

The Major said, rather smugly, "Oh, I might not have seen her but I may yet have a record of her passing this way today." He beckoned to me to follow him and admitted us to one of his sheds where he somewhat surprised me by switching on an electric globe. However, on reflection I suppose it would be a poor sort of photographic scientist who did not take advantage of each new invention. His air was somewhat secretive as he closed the door behind us and reached onto a shelf for a small rectangular box that he explained to me contained an exposed roll of film. As a mere layman (albeit one with interest which causes me to read some weekly and monthly publications rather beyond the scope of *The Strand*) I had heard of the newly-introduced roll film which it was claimed would soon replace both glass plates and cut film in photography. He explained to me that he had designed and built a special camera which would not only operate on such rolls of film but would move the film through a series of weights and pulleys so that the photographer would not need to move the film by hand at all. He showed me diagrams and explained that his roll films were manufactured for him expressly by a firm called Kodak. There were a number of boxes on the shelf, each dated for a different day of the week and month. He further explained that the negatives bore a ready printed date. "I use a fresh roll each day and always know the exact date each picture is taken. I am working now upon a further development which will incorporate a clock in the camera which will record the time of the making of the exposure."

The Major switched off the light bulb in the box and turned on another which was of a greenish hue, saying, "Most of my contemporaries use a red bulb in the darkroom but I have found this particular shade to be even safer. Well now Sir, I will develop the film and we can see if your missing old woman appears upon it." I had to admit that this was a useful idea but protested that the process might be rather time consuming as I had an appointment. Having been assured that the Major's methods were photographically speaking extremely economical with time I agreed to stay and watch the developing process.

During the Afghan campaign I had once been invited into the portable darkroom of a newspaper photographer to watch him develop a glass plate which he had taken for the benefit of his readers and this had eventually appeared after a series of time consuming processes to depict a rather stuffy looking group of officers and their native servants, stiffly posed in front of a bell tent, but I soon realised that the Major had indeed left those days and their methods behind. He first unrolled the film and stripped the film itself from its paper backing. He then attached a heavy metal clip to each end of the celluloid and suspended it into what appeared to be a sort of converted drain pipe, filled with nauseous looking liquid. He remarked, "It will take but a few minutes to develop, then after I have fixed and washed it you will be able to see it in the normal light ..." He shook the drainpipe from time to time, a manoeuvre which he referred to as agitation.

After what seemed like an hour, but was in fact but a few minutes, the film strip was removed from the pipe full of developer and lowered into another which I was assured was full of a solution of hypo. "That fixes it y' know, only takes a minute or two. Then while I'm washing the chemicals away you will be able to see it."

I will spare the reader further photographic technicalities and explain that under a running tap in a sink the film was spread out for my inspection. There amid other images in negative was that of old Maude, complete with her handcart. I gasped and enquired, "What time do you consider this image of the old woman to have been captured?" His reply was immediate, "Not one of the pictures was taken before midday, for at that time I loaded the camera. Judging by the state of the light I would estimate that it was taken between two thirty and three of the clock."

As the Major hung the strip of film by its top clip in a sort of steel cupboard from which heat seemed to emerge I found my mind racing around to try and accept the fact that old Maude had been wandering around the lawn with her handcart at a time when I had considered it necessary to mount my expedition. I decided to take the chance of asking if I might have, or at least borrow, the Major's negative. He very quickly and obligingly agreed to my request, clipping the portion of film that interested me from the strip with a pair of scissors. He placed it in an envelope that I pocketed thankfully. From politeness I felt it prudent to enquire, "Is there any sign of Dr. Crippen yet Major" He gazed at me keenly, as if examining my expression for signs of ridicule. Evidently finding none he smiled and said, "Why no, but I am sure that given time he will appear when the time is right for him to do so."

Upon my return to number thirty-nine Hilldrop Crescent I could at first find no sign of my friend Sherlock Holmes. But I eventually discovered him, fast asleep, in my camp bed. I did not disturb him, knowing that he had passed perhaps forty-eight hours without sleep, or place to do so in any comfort. But after, about an hour Holmes joined me in a cup of tea that

I had taken the opportunity to brew as he slumbered. "Ah Watson, I see you are back from your expedition. Did you find out anything of use or interest concerning old Maude?" I tried to keep any sort of smugness out of the tone of my reply as I poured my friend a steaming mug of tea. I remarked, as casually as I could, "Not a great deal, save that she is still alive."

Sherlock Holmes had been in the act of raising his tea to his lips as I completed this sentence. He lowered the cup and demanded, "Are you sure; have you seen her, or have you any other evidence to substantiate your statement?" I took the negative from my pocket and laid it before him, placing it upon a sheet of white notepaper from my writing case. This enabled him to more clearly see the negative image and transfer it to positive in his mind. But Holmes lifted it clear of the paper and tilted it in the light, showing me how much easier it was to view that way. "You see Watson, how the emulsion transforms itself to the positive as you tilt it. This is obviously one of the pictures taken by our friend the Major, but as it was taken at a time earlier than this day it can help us little."

I felt rather hurt by the way he seemed to airily dismiss what I felt to be an important piece of discovered evidence. and demanded rather than asked, "The film has been dated, so it is current is it not?"

Holmes smiled grimly as he said, "Watson, it is not difficult to scratch a date on unexposed film, and whoever does this can scratch any date he pleases upon the film can he not?"

I was sceptical, and I wanted my findings to be of moment. I said, "The film is dated by the firm who supply it."

Holmes all but scoffed, "Oh come, look at the writing. It would be the easiest thing in the world to purchase an undated film then doctor it and substitute it. You are far too trusting Watson. I have warned you of this before."

I thought of all the time that I assumed he considered me to have wasted. I was angry both with myself, and my friend, as I all but snapped, "You explain how this seeming date forgery could have been managed, but you do not explain why, or that it is so." My friend lifted the negative and waved it under my nose, saying, "Use your eyes Watson, and you will notice that in this image the old woman is wearing the glittering tiara which has been hanging from a nail in the café for these many hours. The Major has attempted to deceive you, but for reasons which I as yet have no understanding, but cheer up my dear fellow, for you have alerted us to the fact that the Major is not the jolly eccentric we took him for. Though what possible connection that he can have with the matters which we are investigating I fail to see."

I could not explain quite how or why I felt that dark shadows were gathering.

Chapter Five

Belle Elmore

The reader will recollect that contacting and questioning Mr. Clarkson Rose was one of the tasks that had fallen to my lot whilst Sherlock Holmes followed his mysterious (even to myself) investigations. To contact my quarry was a fairly easy task because theatrical performers are inclined to make themselves available to those who wish to engage them. From the advertisement that he had placed in *The Era* it was possible to deduce that he was quite well established and successful. The fact that it was in a column of *Artiste's Cards* it could be judged to be one that had been placed in series, moreover the address was one in Kensington and there was a telephone number. Of course had Holmes been with me he could have suggested that Mr. Rose might be using the address and telephone number of a friend, or be staying at a boarding house, but as soon as I spoke upon the telephone with Rose I realised this not to be so. He had a reassuringly proprietorial air in his rich, fruity voice, unhurried was he in his manner and not irritated when he heard the purpose of my enquiry. I presented myself without the alias that I had used at Hilldrop Crescent and its surrounds.

"Do be seated Dr. Watson, some tea will arrive in a few minutes. Meanwhile I will try to recall anything of moment that I can remember concerning poor Belle. She was quite a nice lady you know, very generous and much loved by her fellow professionals. I mention this first because the journalists tended to paint a rather different picture of her."

As he spoke to me Clarkson Rose stood before a huge portrait of himself in character as a *grande dame*. I could see that the portrait was of the style used as front of the house publicity. Rose seemed a little surprised that I recognised his portrait for what it was, so I explained, "Although an excellent likeness it borders upon the caricature. A nice oil painting, but a little garish, not fine, whilst everything else in your sitting room is in perfect taste." He had an infectious smile this bespectacled and plump young man. He chuckled, "I am no connoisseur but I know what I like Doctor."

Our preliminary banter was interrupted by the entrance of a parlour maid with the tea tray and almost immediately followed by that of a strong featured young woman who was introduced to me as Miss Olive Fox, alias Mrs. Clarkson Rose, "who always plays my idle son, Aladdin, in pantomime."

It is not my intention to burden my reader with details of any small talk that ensued between the three of us. As Andrew Ducrow would have said, 'I'll cut the cackle and get to the horses'.

Mr. Rose was able to dispel the picture painted by the press at the Crippen trial of a fading or untalented performer. He said, "She might not have been exactly star material Doctor, but she was an able soubrette and comedienne. I had enough confidence in her in fact to offer her a twelve-week engagement with my concert party, Twinkle, on condition that she made me a promise concerning her one weakness. She was inclined to be a little too fond of the bottle. But I had said to her 'Belle, if you give me your word that you can be relied on, the season is yours'. She was really looking forward to it and making every effort to keep sober."

Mrs. Rose, or Miss Fox as evidently she could be called, was equally generous in remembering Belle Elmore, "A really very generous woman Dr. Watson. That generosity took the form of the organisation of charity concerts, tirelessly giving her time and abilities to so many good causes. For this reason her death and its circumstances brought great sorrow among members of our profession, especially the ladies, whose organisations she had helped so much. Clarkie and I knew that she was planning to take a cure for her alcoholic problem after which she would have joined us in Twinkle at Scarborough."

I asked them both if they had blamed Crippen for her problems and they both agreed that this was a difficult question to answer though they were inclined to think that Belle would have been more than a match for him in an argument. Eventually we ran out of questions concerning Belle Elmore and I left Clarkson Rose and his wife feeling that I had a point or two that Holmes would find to be of interest.

On the doorstep I asked the Roses one last question, "What are your feelings concerning Ethel le Neve?" They agreed that when they had met her, with Belle, she had seemed a very quiet and well-behaved girl with whom Belle had appeared to be on quite friendly terms.

As I made my way back to Hilldrop Crescent I suddenly realised that neither Clarkson Rose nor Olive Fox had asked me why I had asked them my questions about Belle Elmore. This fact suddenly caused me considerable thought. It was as if they had half expected someone to ask them these questions.

I found Holmes minus his tramp disguise, shaved, washed and dressed as if for a walk in Hyde Park. He said, "Watson, do not look so surprised, you surely knew that I was not destined to walk this earth disguised as a down-and-out forever. Lestrade will be here shortly with some proper food from a decent restaurant. There will also be a decent bottle of claret. When the food and wine is here and we are enjoying it, then and only then will you tell me of your interview with Clarkson Rose and his wife, Olive Fox."

I realised at once that I had not at any point mentioned Olive Fox, or indeed even known of her existence until I had arrived and spoken with them both. I said, "How did you know about Rose's wife?" Holmes said, mysteriously, "Come, let us wait for the relaxation of food and drink." I said, "Holmes, please don't trifle with me. You have asked, nay demanded, my aid with a seemingly pointless project for the reason of which I changed my professional plans at not inconsiderable inconvenience but please do not try me further by adopting a patronising manner towards me."

I believe the arrival of Lestrade with food and drink (the former still hot from an obviously nearby source) prevented the first quarrel that my friend and I would have had. Holmes placated me as he served a splendid meal for the three of us with the air of an expert waiter, considering the conditions in which we would need to consume it. Then he said, "My dear fellow, I will explain. You left behind your copy of *The Era*. It was the work of seconds for me to look for and find the advertisement placed therein by Clarkson Rose, which I knew you would also have found. As my eye ran down the rest of that particular column I noticed a similarly styled advertisement under the name Olive Fox. I was observant enough to note that the telephone number and address were the same as Rose's. No doubt once you had found the name and details you were seeking you did not look any further."

As we sampled the *crêpe suzette* and washed it down with the claret I filled Holmes and Lestrade in upon all that I had learned at the Rose *ménage*. Eventually Holmes said, "We already knew of Belle Elmore's intemperate habits from that which you learned from old Maude, but I had not realised this had taken a form extreme enough for her to require to take a cure. Also although we had read in various reports of her popularity within her profession we now know that this was partly through her extreme generosity. I am also very intrigued with the view of Ethel le Neve that you say was expressed by Clarkson and Mrs. Rose. All the news reports have hinted at her being some sort of scarlet woman. You have done well Watson, you have in fact done rather more than well."

It was my friend's turn to inform me of any discovery or progress that he might have made during my absence. I noticed that despite his seeming hunger in disposing of the main course he had merely played with the rather splendid desert. I made some coffee, and he gratefully took down lung fulls of the Scottish mixture. When he was ready he said, "Watson I cannot claim to have had as fruitful a day as yours has been, but none the less a few interesting facts have emerged. You know Crippen had a son who was only vaguely mentioned at the trial and in reports. But a down and out learns quite a lot if he listens to the gossip of his fellows. I had not realised it, but the son stayed here at around the date of the tragedy." I asked, "Are you suggesting that the son was actually the murderer?"

Holmes replied "No Watson, but I have to consider all possibilities until we have established the pattern of events."

Lestrade had been listening to all that we had been saying. Now he spoke, "I spent some time at the Yard today Mr. Holmes. With the Doctor and yourself doing so much I just felt that I should be doing something to help. Now as you both know I no longer have any sort of official position or power there, but I still have a few friends in the building and I told one of them, Sergeant Dawkins, that I wanted to know the present whereabouts of a certain party."

Holmes said, "Before you go any further Lestrade please assure me that you have not divulged my present interest and activities concerning the Crippen case?"

The ex-Inspector reassured my friend, "Why Mr. Holmes, you know I have more sense than that, I merely said that I had a pal in Fleet Street, writing an article who wanted to know the whereabouts of this certain party."

I could not help but interrupt with an enquiry, "Was the party Crippen's son?" He replied, "No Doctor, it was Ethel le Neve that I was interested in. If this was a proper case, under my control, she would be the next party that I would be interested in."

Holmes's eyes widened and he said, "I confess that Miss le Neve would not have been my very next interest Lestrade, but if you have obtained any information regarding her present activities I would be more than interested to hear about it."

Lestrade, seemingly unable to leave his old ways back at Scotland Yard despite his retirement, pulled himself up to his full height and took a notebook from his jacket. In a very official tone he said, "Well evidently after the trial, not Crippen's, I mean her own, where she was found not guilty, she obtained employment at a well known store in Oxford Street, where she presently sells perfume and other ladies toilet goods such as rouge and face powder. The store is called Selfridges, and she is known there as Ethel Niven. She has even adapted her vocal tones to suit her new Scottish personage. In other words Sir, she speaks with a Scots accent."

Holmes rejoined, "So you have even been to the store and observed her Lestrade?"

The old Yard warhorse said, "I certainly have Sir, even bought some rouge for my wife, though goodness knows what she will do with it."

I chuckled but Holmes was seriously considering Lestrade's words. However, he eventually remarked with a certain joviality, "The gift may bring back a certain amount of popularity to you Inspector, following the recent slight rift between you."

Lestrade started, saying, "Oh, come on Mr. Holmes, how did you know about the bust up between the wife and myself? I have told no one about it." Holmes seemed surprised that he had been asked to explain, "You know Lestrade a wife does not usually allow her husband to sally forth for three days with his shoes dust-and-mud-bespattered."

Lestrade knew better than to question Sherlock Holmes any further concerning this demonstration of his methods. There would have been a time when it would not have been so easily dismissed. But we had more important matters to discuss than the domestic situation at *chez* Lestrade.

Holmes suggested that I renew my friendship with the Major. "Watson, I have today tripped his flashlight and therefore will be interested to learn if I appear upon his roll of film. If I do not it will bear weight to my belief in his adulteration of his own date and time records. Old Maude continues to be missing and sooner or later we must investigate that matter also."

I did as he suggested and again seeking the Major's presence I wandered through the partly-mown grass in the direction of the huts.

I was fortunate to find the Major standing in the open door of his hut that was to my right as I strode towards it. This was the hut in which he had shown me the photographic processes.

He greeted me brightly, "Colonel, we meet again!" (He had taken to addressing me as a colonel, a rank to which I had never risen nor yet aspired to, but then he, I felt sure, had never been a major!). I returned his greeting as heartily as I could, then asked him, "Any sign of Crippen yet?" I had decided that it was easiest and best to humour his obvious mental malady and always speak as if Crippen was quite likely to walk across the lawn at any time.

He bade me enter the shed as he held up yet another roll of film with its neat row of exposures. "No, but our poor old friend Maude has again been picked up." Sure enough there was old Maude, complete with tiara but there was no shot of Holmes.

I enquired, "When did you remove the film?"

He replied, "About an hour ago." I then made the mistake of consulting my hunter. He took note of this and asked, sharply, "Do you have an appointment Colonel? If so I must not keep you."

I managed to cover my foolish action by saying that I had left a saucepan on a low heat at my home. I did not feel at the time that he suspected any significance in my lapse. But now of course I knew that Holmes had been right about the adulterated dating on the films, through his own non-appearance on this one and old Maude's presence: wearing the tiara which would certainly not have been detected, unless everything was far more complicated than I suspected it to be.

For the first time I noticed, as I prepared to depart, that the other shed had a small chimney, rather as you would see on the roof of a gypsy cart or caravan. Some smokes wisps were emerging from it. A rather strange odour could also be detected but I assumed that the Major was preparing some sort of witches brew connected with his photographic experiments.

Back at number thirty-nine, Sherlock Holmes showed great interest in my findings. "So you were shown another roll of film with false dating, showing that which could not have been on it and not showing that which should. It would indeed be interesting to know what the actual and correctly dated film did show, aside from an image of myself." Then Holmes surprised me considerably by announcing, "I have to depart for Fowlhaven this very evening Watson. There is little you can do here for the moment and I suggest that you return to your home, there to stay for a day or two, and I will contact you there upon my return."

I did not wish to pry into the nature of that which had occurred to cause this change of plan, feeling that Holmes would inform me of it if indeed he so wished to do. However, I did feel suspicious and wondered if Fowlhaven was where Holmes was actually going, or whether it was merely a further ruse to allow him to continue another line of investigation into the Crippen affair. As it happened there were matters of my own that required dealing with and a forty-eight hour interval in our current investigations would suit both of us very well.

I asked, "Does Lestrade know?" Holmes nodded to signify that the good ex-Inspector of police had been made familiar with the situation. As our directions of travel differed I took a taxicab to my home, leaving Holmes to the mercies of Lestrade, who, I was informed, would call presently for him with the motor car.

When I arrived back home I first took full advantage of my various means of creature comfort. A hot bath, a complete change of clothing as well as a better shave than I had been able to for these last days. There were then a few letters to be attended to and a report from my locum upon the progress that he had attained concerning Mrs. Lowther's lumbago. My servant wished me goodnight and I settled down to what I considered a well-earned rest in my favourite armchair. I even dozed a little from sheer fatigue. But I could not contemplate going to bed whilst my mind was quite so active. That which we had learned played through my brain. It had of course all started with Holmes's sudden interest in the Crippen murder and he seemed to me to be the only person who had ever voiced any sort of possibility concerning any doubt as to Crippen's guilt. Why otherwise would he and le Neve in her bizarre and rather clumsy disguise have attempted to leave the country so swiftly and without informing anyone which could only seem to suggest guilt. Belle Elmore had been painted by the press as some sort of drunken harridan, a variety artiste of very little talent, yet we had learned that this was not an entirely accurate summation of her abilities or behaviour. Clarkson Rose and his wife had suggested that she was both clever and kindly, as had old Maude, to whom she had evidently given a valuable diamond studded tiara. My discovery of bones in the attic had done little either to afford any encouragement to Holmes's view of the vague possibility of innocence. As for the adventures concerning the Major and his wrongly dated photographs, these seemed to me to be unconnected with the Crippen affair save in his extremely bizarre view that Crippen would reappear in ghostly form. As for the defrocked cleric with the soup kitchen and very ungodly views, why there seemed to be little connection save that he had occupied thirty-nine Hilldrop Crescent before Crippen.

I had to admit to myself that however unlikely Crippen's innocence might be there were points of the case that did seem to need some sort of clarification.

As I sat and mused upon these facts and conjectures in the comfort of my own living room I yet felt a sudden guilt because of this very lethargy to which I had returned. I knew not the nature of the matter that had called Holmes away and began to feel that I should do something towards our investigations lest I feared that my friend might have suggested my withdrawal from the fray because he sensed that my interest had waned somewhat. But what to do in his absence that might help him, there was the rub!

Then suddenly I knew what I should do. I might be using my time to advantage if I investigated the latest activities of the dubious parson. With this in mind I decided to follow Holmes's example and to present myself at the church in the disguise of a tramp or down and out. I could not hope to match the mastery of my friend in such theatricals, but I felt sure that I would be able to pass unrecognised by the once reverend gentleman.

My first thought then in this direction was sartorial. None of my own clothes seemed to have reached the required state of seediness, including those that I wore when directing the workman in my garden. Then I remembered some garments that had been destined for the attentions of the dustman; old, and given great attention from the moths. I found the sack, fortunately as yet uncollected, and indeed for once I rejoiced in the slothful habit of the British working man: I had soon assembled a disgustingly moth-eaten pair of tweed trousers, some boots that I had worn on various fishing expeditions, a jacket that had been burned by accident when being ironed by a housemaid who had been instantly dismissed for the offence, and a bowler hat which had become mildewed in a damp cupboard.

Having made this selection I started to ill treat the garments in order to even further mar their appearance. The hat was easy to stove in, and the boots not difficult to scuff with a variety of household implements. The trousers I made almost tattered and the burnt jacket required very little work from me. It was easy enough to stain a shirt and wear it minus its collar, and a duster from the kitchen worn as a neckerchief completed the picture save for the final touches. With soot from the fireplace I managed to make my face look unshaven, and by combing out the wax from my moustache and trimming it on one side only I felt I had created the perfect Albert Bloggs!

Of course in my excitement in creating a caricature of myself I had forgotten one important fact: I had to get myself to Holloway and I doubted if any cab rank would make me welcome. I pondered on this dilemma. Of course, the answer to it soon came to me. I would rouse my servant and send him to fetch a cab, with some invented excuse and warning concerning my eccentric appearance.

Fortunately Hargreaves lived upon the premises, so it was not difficult to rouse him. But I had quite overlooked his own reaction to being awakened by such an apparition!

The poor faithful fellow would have caused me laughter had it not concerned such an important incident, and the fact that he grabbed a fire iron from the grate in his room and threatened me with it. "Who are you fellow, and what are you doing in Dr. Watson's house at this hour? By George, your answer had better be a good one!"

I spoke, and fortunately he recognised my voice. "Hargreaves, it is quite alright, I am in disguise." "Upon my word, it is you Doctor, but why are you about at such an hour, and dressed as a dustman down on his luck?"

I explained the situation to him, cutting all corners and telling him only what he really needed to know, including the fact that I required the services of a taxicab. He dressed very quickly and none too carefully, so that the two of us must have together presented a startling picture. As an excuse I told him to tell the taxicab driver that I wished to attend a tramps' ball in the Holloway area. As he left to do my bidding, Hargreaves paused to ask, "Forgive me asking this Doctor, but how are you going to manage the return journey?" (He knew nothing of my temporary shared apartment in Hilldrop Crescent), I simply replied, "I shall handle that problem when I come to it Hargreaves."

When my man returned with the vehicle I noted that the driver did not seem to be exactly delighted with the prospect of driving me, despite the promise of a genuinely generous extra payment. (With this in mind I had remembered to pick up my purse, though not my wallet, and had also decided to carry my service revolver). The fellow said, "I know you toffs likes to dress up like down and outs now and then and I suppose its your idea of fun, but it seems odd to a hard working man like myself who tries hard to keep up appearances. Perhaps you wouldn't mind leaning well back, for I don't want the other cabbies to see you, I may get made into a laughing stock if they do. Imagine, it would be a case of 'Oh Albert, better class of passengers I see' and all that sort of thing." I promised to do as I had been bid.

The journey was not a long one but was far from comfortable for me in my rags, and I contorted to try and avoid being seen as much as was possible. I did this as much for my own benefit as the driver's after a while, for early on some rough young fellows had spotted me and made the most of my incongruous position, as the reader might imagine.

When we reached the general vicinity of the church I bade the driver to let me out of the cab. There were quite a few genuine unfortunates making their way to my destination. As I gave the driver his hefty gratuity he remarked, "Quite a few other nobs and swells going to the tramps' ball I see. I'll tell you this, if there is some sort of prize for most realistic layabout, you'll win hands down guv'nor."

I tried to make my own entrance into the church as quietly as possible. The other, and genuine, unfortunates cast wary eyes in my direction. Some of them muttered various incantations, such as, "They're all gettin' to hear about this place" and "Who told him there'd be pies and no singing?"

The reverend gentleman beamed at me so that had his teeth been false they would have fallen out. He obviously, to my immense relief, failed to recognise me, saying, "Welcome my son, all are welcome here." I nodded and mumbled as I entered the church. There were some half a hundred unfortunate souls who quickly went to where they usually sat by habit, or so I assumed. I was very careful to avoid trying to occupy what might seem like an ideal position for reasons that will be obvious to the reader. But I had neglected one important aspect of my disguise, as I was soon to discover when a dishevelled harridan pointed to my right hand and said, "'ad a manicure 'ave you ducks?" I muttered to the effect that I had dangled my hands in the horse trough, and was quite relieved at my own presence of mind. None the less I soon discovered that there were plenty of dusty corners in the church and I quickly made good use of such grime without calling attention to my actions.

The denizens of the church as I began to think of them were dividing into small groups or huddles with here and there one of them proving to be a complete lone soul. I suppose I passed as one of these as I crouched upon the remains of what once had been a church pew. Then quite suddenly the completely unexpected happened; Sherlock Holmes, in the disguise which I knew so well, entered and made his way unsteadily down the church aisle, towards the altar area, where stood the gently smiling cleric. He laid a calming hand upon Holmes's shoulder, saying, "There, there, Leonard, you must quietly wait, as do the rest of them. The pies will soon be here and later on, as I promised, I shall take you into the back room for a special talk during which we will discuss in some depth your problem to which I feel I have the answer."

I turned to a derelict fellow who stood nearby and asked him, "Does he often take members of this congregation into the back room?"

The fellow said, "Fairly often, and it is my opinion that he does or says something to them which changes the whole course of their lives."

I asked, "What makes you think that?"

His reply rather surprised me; he said, "Why because they never gets seen by any of us again. It's my belief that the minister has the answer to whatever troubles whoever is lucky enough to be called by him. Who can say what happens; a bath, a clean suit of clothes, some large sum of money and a good job in another district."

This remark puzzled me and I enquired, "Why would he send the selected one to a fresh area?"

He looked pityingly at me and said, "Fat lot of good it would do him being made a new man with us lot all hanging around to sponge off him. A fellow would need a new lot of companions of his own class!"

I gasped at the illogic of his words, saying, "Are **we** not of his class?"

Again he was patronising in his reply, "Not any more, but an educated man like yourself could surely work that out?"

Evidently my attempt to speak in plebeian tones had not been a great success. I pondered upon just what my next move should be. Should I simply leave Holmes to his own devices in the assumption that he had anticipated any possibility of danger? The logic of this seemed clear enough, for I had no proven reason to suspect that any sort of peril lay in the backroom; just a feeling that it might.

I mused that the fact the cleric had been defrocked did not in itself suggest that he was a danger to anyone. Perhaps he really did find new pastures and new lives for members of this flock from sheer goodness of heart, and it was possible, that being so, that he had seen the good in Holmes that disguise had attempted to cover? The other side of the coin did of course occur to and present itself to me. Perhaps something of a sinister nature had happened in that little back room to each of those who had been thought to have been chosen for good fortune? If this were the case my friend might at this very moment be in deadly danger. Having spent a few minutes weighing all the possibilities in my mind I started to move toward the closed door behind the altar.

Chapter Six

The Back Room

The door to my great surprise did not resist my attempt to open it. But as soon as I was beyond it the door slammed behind me, activated through the efforts of the Major. Holmes was already restrained by a rope tying his hands behind him. The 'mad vicar' (as I had secretly come to think of him) stood, holding a knife to my friends side. What to do next? I had only fleeting seconds to decide for as the Major had pushed back the door he had made a wild grab at me, which I of course resisted. I was fortunately able to cast him aside so that he fell to the floor.

As the attentive reader will know, I had decided to bring my service revolver with me on this particular expedition. I blessed the army training which had shown me so well how to quickly present it for use. I managed to swiftly give both of my antagonists the idea that they were to move to the left hand corner of the room as I faced it. They both conveyed their surrender by their passive actions and facial expressions. The Vicar had cast the knife from him and I stooped to retrieve it, being at the same time careful not to take my eyes off my captives. With it I made a rather clumsy job of cutting Holmes free, due to not wishing to transfer the revolver in order to use the knife with my right hand.

As I performed this task Holmes spoke to me with gratitude in his voice, "My dear Watson, I am delighted to see you as you can well imagine."

I expressed surprise that he had so soon managed to recognise me. He said, "Come Watson, you went to quite a lot of trouble with your disguise, which might have deceived if it were not for the sight of your neck. Even with that disgusting hat on I can still recognise the work of your barber. Obviously after all these years you still favour that somewhat military cut when most men, aye and even city men at that, favour somewhat longer hair. I usually can anticipate your actions Watson, but I confess I did not predict that you would undertake this latest and extremely dangerous enterprise of yours. You have amazed me for once Watson. Well, now that we are both here, within the inner sanctum so to speak, you might as well see and hear all that of which I have learned, although I would suggest that you first tie these two scoundrels rather in the style that they meted out to me. Allow me to do the honours with the revolver. It is a long time since you used it, whilst I still undertake regular target practice."

The Major at this point asked, "May I ask what your purpose might be gentlemen in binding and holding us in this way?"

Holmes replied, "Upon charges that you will have the onus of disapproval concerning the intentions which the pair of you held concerning my own person, and which you would have carried out had my friend not put in a welcome appearance. It is obvious that the pair of you meant harm to my person, otherwise you would hardly have restrained and threatened me with a knife."

The vicar spoke in soft tones, "I fear, Sir, that you might find it difficult to prove that we meant you harm, beyond an intention to convey you to another place and there to release you. Our purpose in so doing would have been to rid our happy congregation from contamination with someone whom we consider to be a very bad influence."

I interpolated, "In the same way as you have been regularly ridding your so called congregation from the company of numerous worthies who would obviously have reappeared in this area if some harm had not become them?"

Holmes nodded in agreement, but my words of course had a quite different effect upon the Major, who all but shouted, "My friend here has only to shout to his flock beyond the door to have them force an entry and rescue us both from your meddling, interfering hands. You have nothing to offer save theories in defence of your actions. I suggest therefore that you untie us forthwith that we may get on with the very business that next concerns us, which is the distribution of the pies upon which these poor wretches depend upon for regular nourishment. I suppose you are about to accuse us of poisoning these excellent comestibles?"

Holmes smiled grimly, saying, "No, I make no such suggestion, and yet nothing on earth would make me eat one of them."

It was the Vicar who replied to this, "Come you were happy enough to take one yourself a night or two ago." Holmes said, "But if you had been more observant you would have noticed that I took but a single mouthful, afterwards pocketing the remainder of the pie for later analysis."

I admit that my friend's statement puzzled me at the time, as did his next action that was to fire my revolver into the plaster above us. But I had not much time to ponder following the shock that his action produced. Within a few seconds I heard the blowing of police whistles and the sound of some scuffling from the body of the church. Holmes shouted, "In here Lestrade, through the vestry door!"

Pleased indeed was I to see Lestrade, with another tall man very obviously a high ranking plain-clothes detective, and several burly constables with truncheons at the ready. The congregation could be heard to be in full retreat, wanting little to do with the law. Holmes said, "I'm very pleased to see you Lestrade, and you Inspector Fairbairn. Well, I said that I would give you a signal, but I did not expect it to be of quite such a startling nature; for I was not expecting Watson's timely arrival." He then turned to face me, saying, "My dear fellow, I owe you my life, aye, and not for the first time, for I still awaken sometimes from nightmares concerning my entombment at Sandringham House. Well old friend on that occasion I had left clues for you to follow, but on this present occasion I had no expectation of help. Come, let us leave these rascals in the safe hands of Inspector Fairbairn and return to Hilldrop Crescent."

Lestrade accompanied us to our temporary headquarters and I made haste to brew coffee, hot and strong for the three of us. As we charged our pipes, Holmes explained, "Watson you must not think that I concealed information that I had gained from you for anything but the best of reasons. If I wish to be so foolish as to risk my life through such an escapade, so be it, but I have no right whatever to risk yours. Had I given you the choice I did realise that you would have elected to participate. For this reason I suggested that you should leave the scene for a while, but failing to realise that you would have tried to play me at my own game with your excellent disguise."

I pondered upon his words, having many questions to ask my friend and wondering which should come first. Eventually I asked, "What on earth was all this business about pork pies?" Holmes smiled kindly and said, "The Reverend gentleman feeds his flock, as he calls then, upon so called pork pies, which are actually made from human flesh" – he paused to light his pipe, then continued – "which I suspected were not made of pork but could not be entirely sure of the substitute until I had pretended to sample one but actually had saved it to analyse." I gasped and interrupted his explanation by asking, "You found the pie to be made from the flesh of a human being, and had you suspected as much?"

The horrific nature of the topic under discussion was tempered a little by the quite cold-blooded way in which Holmes discussed it. He reminded me, not for the first time of one of my early medical tutors; the scientific interest outweighing the horrific nature of a disease being discovered in an organ. Holmes the scientist frequently took over from Holmes the human being! His answer was clear, "I could not be sure, for there are many pale substitutes for pork, including poultry, but yes, I had suspected my analysis to confirm my fears."

Holmes worked hard upon his pipe before he continued, "At very regular intervals one of the flock, congregation or whatever you might wish to call them would be called to the vestry, never to be seen again. After they had been despatched to meet their maker they would be dissected in the vestry, their flesh then transferred to one of the two sheds where the actual pie making would take place. One of the sheds, the one you know so well both inside and out was a mere decoy for the grisly activities which took place in the other." He paused again and I took the opportunity to ask questions.

"Have you inspected the inside of the second shed?"

"No Watson, I had asked Inspector Fairbairn to take the opportunity of doing so whilst earlier tonight both suspects would, I imagined, be engaged in the church. Lestrade will no doubt be able to tell you more than I can."

Lestrade took up the narration, "Inside the shed, which I opened with a skeleton key, I found neatly bundled pieces of flesh, which I could not identify as to type, but could see clearly that there were human bones in bins, from which the flesh had been removed, in a seemingly skilled manner."

Holmes nodded, "Thank you Lestrade, and of course also for your more than helpful liaison work which brought in Inspector Fairbairn." Then he turned to address me once more. "Watson, you may wonder what led me to feel that there was something strange about the second shed? Well, for one thing the Major was very open in showing the other shed to you, and explaining all his photographic wonders concerned with his entirely pretended interest in the ghost of the late Dr. Crippen. Also you may recall that the foxes were seen to be showing a singular interest in the shed where the meat was stored, and, I suspect, pie making took place. 'Reynard' is a slim fellow Watson, and does not risk his life in urban areas without anticipation of gains in the shape of meat."

I confessed to being somewhat bewildered as I asked, "But my dear Holmes, what possible motive did an unfrocked priest and an ex-army major have in luring down and outs to their death and concocting such incredibly involved arrangements by which to do so?" Holmes nodded his understanding of my bewilderment.

"Well Watson, and Lestrade, for I can see that you are a little puzzled too, the Major, as he calls himself has, I have discovered, a long history of political activity with an obscure group pledged to reducing the population by extremely unorthodox means. For example at one time they planned to campaign with a certain Dr. Forbes who maintained that all persons should be painlessly destroyed upon reaching the age of sixty-five. As for the Vicar, he has a similar history of bizarre beliefs and campaigns, including an all but unbelievable theory that the poor and needy should reduce their numbers by eating each other."

I considered Holmes's all but unbelievable words before asking, "How did this liaison begin?"

"The Major and the Vicar met when they were both inmates of an institution for the insane in Haywards Heath in Sussex. They discovered some common ground in their insanities and were both very crafty in the pretence of a return to sanity which allowed first the Vicar, and later the Major, to be released. The Vicar was able to take a short lease on this property, but Crippen later moved in forcing the Vicar to another address. These premises are being searched and examined even as we speak. The flesh found in the cellar by the way was more than likely left over from the time when it was used as a dissection area."

This considered opinion of Holmes's was perhaps the most surprising thing that I had experienced during a night of bizarre events. Gradually an all important question occurred to me. I enquired of Holmes, "Do you now consider that the two persons under discussion were responsible for the death of Belle Elmore?" Rather to my surprise my friend shook his head, "No Watson, I believe the only connection is in the occupation of this address and the matter of the mistaken identification of the flesh and hair attributed to be that of Mrs. Crippen, and indeed the only evidence offered as far as a body was concerned. In investigating one horrific crime we have merely turned up another."

There was one point that still worried me and would require a convincing answer from my friend. "Holmes, Crippen and his wife had occupied this property for several years; how then had decay failed to claim those portions of flesh?" Holmes rose from his chair and said, "Pray follow me Doctor, and you will answer that question for yourself." I followed him down the steps and into the cellar. Holmes continued, "Other than our actual surroundings what major difference do you notice between the room we have just vacated and this apartment?"

Of course I almost immediately realised that I was about to answer my own question. I said, "It is several degrees cooler." Holmes replied, "Brilliant Doctor, and as a man of medicine and science you will realise that it is in fact cool enough down here for there to be very little flesh decay: rather like the catacombs which lie below many European cities."

I was grateful that Lestrade had not descended with us when Holmes gave his answer to my question, "I wonder why Scotland Yard did not take that into account at the time of their enquiries?" Holmes's reply, "They had decided that Crippen was guilty before the very fullest investigations had taken place. Remember Watson, he looked like a murderer, but even more against him was the fact that he behaved like one in fleeing with his mistress before any sort of accusation had been made or even considered."

"You still consider then that he was innocent?"

"I still consider the possibility, that is all."

"Yet you have spent so much time upon the matter."

"Oh come Watson, is it not an interesting exercise?"

I had to admit that it was interesting as exercises went, but I still could not see why Holmes was so interested in solving such a case as this one where the principal participant had already been executed. Nothing we could do would bring him back, guilty or not! As for immediate matters, I decided that I would return to my home, at least for long enough to avail myself of the opportunity to dispense with my tramp disguise and obtain a few hours sleep. Lestrade kindly offered to drive me to my home, an offer which I did not refuse as I felt I might find difficulty in finding a cab, due to the lateness of the hour and my attire. Holmes agreed that we would recommence our investigations upon the morrow, saying crustily, "I shall enjoy an undisturbed night upon your camp bed Watson, but please remember that we must make an early start."

Lestrade and I discussed the excitement of the hours past and then began to discuss Holmes's seeming determination regarding the Crippen affair. I said, "Do you not think that Holmes's activities of late have been a little pointless?" He rounded on me a trifle sharply, "Oh come Doctor, do you consider the entrapment and apprehension of two murderers, both insane and capable of who knows how much devilry to be pointless?" Of course I took his point but I added, "Although I of course agree that had we not been involved concerning Crippen these horrific events would have continued to occur, but I was speaking of his seeming obsession to rake over old coals."

As I descended from the car and Lestrade attempted to restart his vehicle he gave me his parting shot. "During the many years that we both have known him, Mr. Holmes has, as I have observed it, helped to make this world a better, safer place for the law-abiding to inhabit. It matters little if he makes some fresh discovery regarding Crippen, for only good comes from his actions and interests. Now Doctor, if you would be so kind as to give the engine another turn?" I revolved the starting handle and the hum of the machinery rewarded my effort. Lestrade waved as he left the scene in a cloud of exhaust fumes. Then I took myself in to my house and as Pepys would have said, 'And so to bed'.

After Lestrade's reprimand I slept the sleep of one who had truly been put in his place, but sleep I certainly did.

It was fully eleven of the clock upon the following morning as I entered thirty-nine Hilldrop Crescent again, to find Holmes absent, although I had not long to wait before he joined me.

"My dear Watson, you are tardy as ever but fortunately my activities have perhaps made up for this. Come, half the morning is gone, there is no time to waste." I began to stutter some sort of excuse but my friend signalled that I should desist from any sort of apology. "Watson, I have breakfasted at top of the bill Berties' establishment, mainly because I wanted to see if old Maude's tiara was still there. Not only was I rewarded to find that it was still hanging upon its hook, but by the sight of old Maude herself, who entered as large as life to reclaim it. I was even able to converse with her over a fourpenny one, and the conversation was quite informative. Crippen had a son ..." I interrupted, "We already know this from the information you have already collected!" Holmes glared at me, "Pray do not interrupt, there's a good fellow; I was about to say that Crippen had a son, as we had already established, and what is more he was very much upon the scene around the time of Belle Elmore's disappearance."

I considered his words and his obvious interest in the fact that the younger Crippen had been on the scene. At length I said, "He was Belle Elmore's stepson was he not, and does he become in your mind a suspect as her possible killer?" Holmes replied, "Not necessarily for that would be jumping the gun a little, would it not?" I remarked, "There was bad blood between them, old Maude has said as much." He said, "I believe there was bad blood between Mrs. Crippen and a number of persons, so I don't think this could make him an automatic suspect, yet it could explain something that has puzzled me. You may remember my bewilderment concerning Crippen's sudden departure from the scene with Miss le Neve, dressing her and passing her off as his son. I have given this very considerable thought and I am coming, not to the conclusion mark you Watson, but simply to the vague possibility that Crippen, far from being the killer suspected that his son might be. His action in departing with the disguised le Neve suggests to me the possibility, yes again just that, of an attempt to lead the authorities away from his son and throw suspicion on to himself. Miss le Neve, who was probably innocent of any sort of involvement must have indeed been fond of Crippen to go along with such a hare brained scheme."

My friend was thrusting upon me surprise after surprise and indeed a growing bewilderment with each fresh suggestion at the path that his mind could be taking. I could accept the possibility of the decoy manoeuvre, yet could remember little mention of the son in the documentation of the Crippen case that Lestrade had supplied, nor in Holmes's perusal of the newspapers of the period. Eventually I asked a perhaps rather obvious question, "Holmes, why did the son not take advantage of the chance to escape, or at the very least make himself scarce?"

Sherlock Holmes smiled enigmatically as he replied, "Perhaps we should consider the possibility of the son being innocent, and yet believing that his father was guilty did not wish to desert him."

I gasped, "So each thought the other to be guilty. This is possible I suppose considering her lack of affection for either of them. But Holmes, if they were indeed both innocent, then who killed Belle Elmore?" He chuckled, "You are thinking we are no nearer to solving the enigma Watson? Well, this is possible, but I would wager that we are a little nearer to discovering the truth than you might suspect. I have only a theory at present, but remember that where there is theory there can also be substance. For the moment, however, there is much to be done if this very strange enigma is to be resolved."

I wondered if this meant that he still required my help, but I did not need to ask the question because he answered it with his own next pronouncement, "Watson, in addition to putting myself in to a situation which almost ended in my demise I have not been idle since you departed for your green suburb. I know we made a rather full search of these premises and came up with very little that was of help. (I ground my teeth remembering the store of male and female bones that I had found in the attic but decided to say nothing). However, before leaving here upon my adventure at the church I made a minor discovery. You will remember that there were practically no furnishings in this house when we took up our residency. Indeed there is even as we speak only those essential items here that you had the foresight to bring with you. But I noticed that there was a cupboard in one bedroom that is in the category known as fixtures. It is screwed to the wall by means of a number of brass fittings, which have been fixed to the back of the cupboard in such a manner that they protrude at the side to present screw holes, by means of which the cupboard is fixed firmly to the wall."

I felt that Holmes was being tedious but said nothing, and as he beckoned to me to follow I did so. He led me to the bedroom in question and pointed dramatically to the cupboard in question, rather like Maskelyne or Devant at St. George's Hall. He said, "Eh *voila!*" I replied, "Well, we did look inside the cupboard and found absolutely nothing save a little dust." Holmes chuckled, "Many a seemingly innocent object can hold its secrets unless it is given more than a mere cursory examination. You will notice Watson that I have removed the screws from the brass fittings. I did this that I might move the cupboard away from the wall. It being little more than a yard high it of course will have supplied the perfect surface upon which its owner could place bills, letters, shopping lists or any of those thousand and one things for which we all seem to find it difficult to find a sensible resting place. There was, as often occurs, a tiny gap betwixt wall and the rear of the cupboard. It is not difficult to imagine how through the years many a folded paper or envelope might have fallen out of view and its loss thought to be of a permanent nature. I found a number of such articles when I moved the cupboard away from the wall."

In a rather dramatic fashion Holmes dropped a transparent packet onto the top of the cupboard. I could see that it contained a number of those very items that my friend had already mentioned. There were, as he showed me, two or three receipts for ladies clothing on the billheads of local shops, likewise a bill from a wine shop in the Holloway Road which had a warning in red ink on its lower edge, suggesting that if the account were not to be settled swiftly legal proceedings would regretfully ensue. Another receipt was for a quantity of henna purchased from a chemist in Islington and a brochure for a hotel in Reigate specialising in what it called 'rest and rehabilitation'. There were sundry other papers and bills which I found of no particular interest.

Holmes asked me, "What do you make of them Watson, for come it is some time since we combined in an exercise using my methods, which you know so well?" I glanced again at some of the papers, at length saying, "Well most of the bills are receipted upon dates well past those upon which they should have been settled. This of course is not unusual in eccentric or chaotic households, which we know that of the Crippen's to have been, as the bills are mostly owing for goods specifically for her own use, for example cosmetic items. The long overdue bill from the wine shop indicates her fondness for drink, but then Holmes this is really just a reiteration of those things already known to us." My friend indicated that we should return to the only room in the house with any sort of comfort involved, but first he asked me to look inside the cupboard, which I did, though finding little of interest.

Holmes lounged as comfortably as he could upon my camp bed whilst I did what I could with the folding chair as we both sough the solace of tobacco. At length he said, "There is something you have not commented upon, in fact two or three things. For example, the receipt for the purchase of henna." I said, "A substance of I believe Egyptian origin, used mainly for the colouration of hair; not an unusual process for women these days." Holmes replied, "Quite so, but do you not consider it a little unusual for a woman of mature years, one who has bleached her hair with a solution of peroxide for a long time to suddenly wish to redden her tresses?" "It had not occurred to me to question that point and I still do not think it is of any interest in our investigations." Holmes nodded wisely in that irritating manner he used when he had a thought of his own that he considered unnecessary to mention, instead asking, "And what do you make of the brochure from the hotel in Reigate?"

From my friend's tone of voice I deduced that he considered this item to be of some interest so I did not give the reply that immediately came to mind. Instead asking, "Do you think it significant?" Sherlock Holmes smiled and said, "You answer my question by asking one in return Watson? Well, in answer to your own enquiry, yes I do consider it to be of more interest than you appear to." I said, "It is merely an advertising brochure extolling the virtues of a country hotel, the sort of thing that most of us receive unsolicited from time to time and usually consign to the waste paper basket!" Holmes nodded, saying, "True Watson, very true, but Mrs. Crippen did not discard it, and at one point it rested on top of the cupboard behind which it accidentally fell. However unimportant it may have become there was at least a short period when it was considered to be of some interest." I could not quite grasp the point that he was trying to make. "Surely you do not think that the Crippens were considering a holiday in Reigate; I base my own doubt upon their animosity towards each other and also the close proximity to London of Reigate. Hardly a holiday resort at that." "Perhaps she had planned to go there alone?" I asked a question without much conviction but to my surprise Holmes said, "I think that could have been quite likely Watson, especially in view of several pawn tickets for articles of jewellery, evidently unredeemed." He dropped a couple of such tickets before me and I had to admit to have scarcely noticed or considered them earlier. I glanced at them again, noting they were from several different pledge offices. I said, "We already knew that Crippen had pawned some of her jewels." Holmes almost snapped, "But these are made out to Mrs. Crippen. Evidently she had quite a few valuable trinkets, some of which he knew of and could put his hands to, and some of which he did not know or could not get at."

What Holmes was saying began to make some sort of a pattern. "You mean she pawned the jewels in order to fund her escape, and planned to stay at this hotel in Reigate?" He nodded, "It seems to me quite likely Watson." I began to say, "And before she could put her plan into action she was murdered." But before I got any answer there was a brisk knocking on the front door. I arose saying, "I wonder if that is Lestrade?" Holmes said, "No, Lestrade has a very distinctive knock, three short knocks and one longer one, rather like the code of Mr. Morse! This is, however, the determined knock of someone who feels that he has every right to be disturbing us." I considered, "The police?" Holmes replied, "No, their knock is usually unmistakable, but I would be inclined to let your manservant in before he thinks there is nobody at home!" I started, "Hargreaves, what the Dickens is he doing here?" I ran to answer the now repeated and somewhat impatient knock and sure enough, upon our doorstep stood Hargreaves.

"Dr. Watson, forgive my intrusion, but you did tell me to contact you at this address in the case of an emergency."

"Yes, man but what on earth could have happened to make you need to contact me so urgently that a telegram would not have sufficed?"

"Well Sir, there has been an outbreak of typhoid fever in Finchley, and you are on the list of those to be consulted at such a time. I thought if I came by taxicab and told the driver to wait you could return with me in it and save some time."

"Typhoid! You have done well Hargreaves, just await my return with my cloak."

Chapter Seven

The Epidemic

I should explain to the reader that I was at that particular time upon a committee that met at once in the event of just such a medical emergency as that with which I was now confronted. Holmes at once offered to accompany me in case he could be of possible help. I appreciated and accepted his kind offer and expressed my thanks to him as the taxicab travelled towards Finchley at a speed that would once have been considered terrifying. My friend brushed aside my thanks, saying, "Watson I not only insist on helping you because you are my best, indeed only, friend, but also for the more obvious reason that you have spared so much of your valuable time in helping me with an investigation which I suspect you consider rather pointless. Well, whilst I do not have your medical knowledge I am a trained observer and might be of some small help."

Holmes was at his most irritating when he ironically played down his own enormous knowledge of science and chemistry, and brilliant powers of observation. I was glad to have him with me as we made for the Finchley town hall. A clerk took us quickly to the office of the local chief medical officer, Dr. Simpson. As we entered his office I saw that it was occupied with several other local doctors known to me. I introduced Sherlock Holmes and those introductions got very mixed receptions. However, most of those present were more deeply concerned with the local serious problem than with meeting a renowned detective.

Simpson was poring over a large-scale map of the area that showed the reservoir of locally stored water. He said to me, "You see Watson, we have been studying this map to see if we can trace any water source that enters the storage lake. You can see the various springs are indicated, which are all known to us as being natural sources of pure water, but can you see a possibility of a contamination source?" I had to admit that I could not and was told that all the marked sources had been tested for purity, or the lack of it. Holmes asked if he might be allowed to examine the map, a request that was granted somewhat grudgingly I thought.

"What are these patches of water quite a way north of the reservoir?" My friend pointed to two or three small areas of blue upon the map. He was informed that these were ponds or small lakes belonging to a market garden. Simpson said to Holmes, "We all know that typhoid is spread through water; but these ponds are mainly there for purposes of irrigation."

Holmes insisted on spending the night at my home. I was of course delighted to have his support and company, but felt a pang of guilt, "Will it not be holding up your own investigation?" He smiled grimly as he said, "Watson your problem is one of life and death for a great many people, whereas with my own the deaths have already occurred, or so it would seem. No, I will put my own efforts at your disposal and together I feel sure we can find the source of the outbreak. I feel equally certain that you can lend me some pyjamas and an old pair of slippers?"

I was able to do even better by lending my friend a dressing robe almost as faded as one of his own, though of blue rather than crimson. As we smoked a final pipe before turning in he was still poring over my own local maps, which were comprehensive enough even if on a somewhat smaller scale than those at the town hall. At length he rose from my second armchair to say, "Watson, I hardly need to remind you that typhoid is mainly spread through continued contact with the original source of infection, rather than being highly contagious from person to person. Therefore we must find that source, and when we do the outbreak will quickly cease. What do you make of this line just near the ponds which you tell me belong to a market garden?" I looked over the map as he held it out. I said, "As far as I can see it is a water pipe but of course it is not marked as such." Holmes snapped, "It is not marked at all." I countered, "I fail to see its significance as it does not empty into the reservoir nor yet into any of the market gardeners' ponds." He nodded, "Quite so Watson, but we must check all possibilities."

Holmes's next action somewhat startled me. He suddenly removed the robe he was wearing and reached for his clothes which were upon a hanger, ready for Hargreaves to sponge and press. He ordered me, "Get dressed Watson, the game is afoot!"

I could not believe that Holmes had suddenly decided that we should instigate some manner of action at such an hour as one o'clock in the morning. I said, "Surely we should wait until morning?" He said, "Certainly not Watson, waste a single hour and you may be wasting another life. If we discover what I think we might find your outbreak could be all but over."

Of course Sherlock Holmes could not be persuaded by matters of practicalities. I asked him, as an example, how we were going to reach the market garden at such an hour. He said, "Watson, we will walk if we have to, for it cannot be more than a couple of miles." But as it happened we did not have to do this as in the old stable I had two bicycles; my own and that which had belonged to my late wife. My own machine was in quite good order because I had often made urgent house calls with it, but Mary's old machine was in a rather shaky condition not having been used for some number of years. Holmes soon got the feel of my bicycle and there was nothing for me to do but climb on the ladies model 'Raleigh' and pedal in his wake. Efficient as ever Holmes had the map, my lens, and a number of other things from my bench, including some tweezers and a supply of transparent specimen bags stored safely in the basket on the front of my magnificent 'Roadster'.

We had a little difficulty with the lamps on the cycles, due to the fact that most of my own journeys by bicycle had been undertaken in daylight, but Holmes insisted that we would meet with little traffic, or even people, at such an hour in the morning. I prayed for him to be right and so it transpired. We reached the market garden in record time and dismounted at the entrance gates. I was all for ringing a bell to announce our presence and stating our business, but there appeared to be nobody around, not even a night watchman, though there was a 'Beware of the Dog' notice. We decided to risk making our entrance without official blessing, leaving the bicycles outside the locked gate that was easy to climb.

I noticed that Holmes had unstrapped the basket from the front of the bicycle, and had also brought the removable battery lamp that although intermittent would throw some sort of light, if emergency should make it needed. We followed the gravel path and could see the various crop beds to our left that sloped away quite sharply. As for the situation to our right, well for the first hundred yards or so we saw nothing much save undergrowth but this eventually gave way to a clear run, revealing a quite substantial pipe running parallel with the path. Holmes observed, "There is our mystery depiction from the map Watson, some kind of water pipe." Taking the lamp and my lens he began to examine the pipe. With some difficulty he managed to read some words that had been impressed upon the metal during manufacture. My friend read the words with some difficulty, turning his eyes into veritable slits as he made out, 'Chalk Farm Sewage Company'. "What do you make of that Watson?" I said, "Just that it is a sewage pipe, carrying waste matter out to the sewage farm which is about two miles to the west of where we stand." He nodded, then asked, "As a medical man would you consider it to be wise to have a sewage pipe running through a market garden?" I replied, "It does not run through the garden, it merely runs along its perimeter, it is nowhere near the items which grow here. Anyway, it appears to be perfectly sealed and sound." As I half expected Holmes said, "A thing though is not always what it appears to be."

We were interrupted at this point not by human agency but by the sudden appearance of a huge dog. Remembering the old adage of the barking dog which never bites I was anxious when it uttered only snarls, showing its teeth in a most terrifying manner. It made a leap at Holmes who managed to grasp one of its forepaws. This appeared to completely immobilise the animal. I remembered reading in some old book of folklore that a dog cannot bite if one of its paws is held in this fashion. I had always dismissed this as being allied to an old wives tale but now that I had seen a demonstration I had to admit that it was practical. However, I was now extremely worried as to what might happen when my friend was forced to release the dog's foot. Holmes though seemed extremely calm for a man about to have his throat ripped open by an Alsatian wolfhound! He said, "Do not worry Watson, I know what to do next, but I do not wish you to witness it so will you kindly avert your gaze?" Obediently I looked away: there was a blood curdling scream followed by a whimper of pain, and when I again turned my head the dog was racing away from us, whining in a truly pitiful manner. I was horrified as I rounded on Holmes, asking, "What unspeakable cruelty did you mete out upon that poor dumb beast?" He chuckled, "It was just an old trick that I learned from llama herders in Tibet for use when attacked by wolves. That poor dumb beast was about to tear me asunder Watson, and he will have fully recovered from my action within minutes, whereas my own career could have been ended forever." I asked, "If what you did was humane why did you ask me to look the other way?" His answer was typical and irritating. He said, "Had you witnessed the Tibetan secret you might have recorded it in one of your scribblings for *The Strand*. Watson I may not be a dog lover, but I am a humanitarian."

I dropped my questioning of his action but continued to cast an eye over my shoulder from time to time as we continued our investigation of the sewage pipe. At length we noticed a watery trickle running across the path, with Holmes at once throwing the shaky light beam at the pipe. It revealed a small crack from which water was undoubtedly causing the slim watery stream that seeped across the path. Holmes turned his attention to the direction that the trickle was taking.

"You see Watson, it makes its way slowly but inevitably down hill into that very wet land section which I assume to be a bed for the growing of watercress." He clambered down from the path and then carefully transferred some of the green spear shaped clusters into a specimen bag by means of the tweezers. Of course I understood instantly what was in his mind. If the sewage leak was infecting the watercress bed then here was the obvious source of the typhoid outbreak.

Later back at my home I tested Holmes's specimen, examining it under the microscope to discover that it was my firm medical opinion that the watercress was capable of infecting anyone who consumed it with typhoid fever. It was obvious that the watercress bed was heavily infected for although the trickle from the sewage pipe was a small one that had gone unnoticed it had undoubtedly been infecting the bed for a long time. The only surprising thing was that the outbreak had not happened very much earlier.

I was amazed at the ignorance shown by some of the members of the medical committee, some of whom could not believe that the outbreak had been caused by infected watercress, but I was happily able to make our point with the result that the market garden was forced to close pending an examination of the sewage pipes. The outbreak soon dwindled away, and I pray that this terrible lesson has been learned.

This unexpected interlude had been both interesting and in its way exciting but I realised that Sherlock Holmes, without whom the typhoid epidemic might not have been tamed, was anxious to get back to his investigation regarding the Crippen case. Our return to Holloway was uneventful, Holmes having requested me to pack another suit of clothes. Naturally I was anxious to know why, because our adventures at Hilldrop

Crescent had not thus far included any social engagements. But he explained.

"Watson I want you to bring with you an extra suit which is in such a state of wear that a smart professional man like yourself would hardly wear it further, and yet a suit that would at a glance appear perfectly respectable. I have a role for you which will require such clothing."

I found such garments as he required, wear that Hargreaves had planned to send to a charity sale at the local church hall. I was indeed puzzled as to this role that I must play, wearing a suit of clothing which I would have been happy enough to wear just a couple of years earlier. I was soon to learn to my consternation just what my role was to be.

However, first, back at Hilldrop Crescent Holmes was to inform me regarding his latest conclusions regarding his investigations in the direction of Dr. Crippen. He said, "Now that you have settled the cause of the typhoid epidemic I feel that your part in that matter is over. The information you have given the authorities should enable them to require your services no longer. There is still work to be done concerning Crippen but that matter too is drawing toward its close. The case of the twentieth century cannibals is almost as incidental as this irritating hold up you have just experienced. Now we must proceed, and swiftly too, before the trail grows cold. I believe my main interest now must concern the hotel brochure from Reigate. As far as I can ascertain Watson, the place is a haven for those who are suffering from extreme cases of alcoholism. We know that Belle Elmore suffered from an overindulgence of this kind, and so it is possible that she was a patient or guest, whichever term you prefer to use, at that establishment."

I said, "Well surely it should not be difficult to contact the establishment and enquire if Belle Elmore had stayed there?" Holmes replied, "Not that simple Watson, you have noted from the brochure the words 'every confidence extended to guests' and of course she would hardly have enrolled under her own name, or I should say any of her own names. All we have to go on is a photograph or two, and the fact that she had probably changed her hair colouring to red by way of the henna that she purchased."

I was about to ask how she would have been able to afford an obviously expensive treatment and accommodation when I remembered the unredeemed pledges that we had also discovered. Instead I simply muttered, "So that is why she pawned the jewellery?" Holmes did not answer, assuming that I had intended to answer my own question. Instead he started to inform me regarding the role that he was expecting me to play. "Watson I will take you with me to the hotel and I will tell them that you are my cousin, a hopeless alcoholic and that you were recommended by an ex-patient. We will show those in charge a photograph of Belle Elmore and see if this will extract any information. For your alcoholic role you will need to dress in your discarded suit and utilise your acting ability to play the rather easy role of a drunkard."

I cannot possibly try to deceive the reader into thinking that the role he had cast me in pleased me in any way whatever, and I was just about to express this in words when I remembered how instant had been Holmes's response in helping me over the matter of the typhoid outbreak. He had not needed to be asked for his help but had assumed that it would be accepted. So I simply gave a nod and said, "All right Holmes, when do we start out for Reigate then?"

Probably the reader has never needed to accompany a drunken friend or relative to somewhere that he or she did not wish to go, but having had an unfortunate brother who was afflicted by such a problem I had a rough idea that it would take more than one attendant to make it convincing. I said, "I suppose Lestrade will join us on our trip to Reigate?" Holmes said, "Watson your supposition is a correct one, and we will of course need to give you a touch of authenticity."

Holmes applied a little rouge from his make up box to my nose and cheeks after he had disarrayed my rather worn apparel, and assured me that on the way he would stop and apply the finishing touches. We travelled to Reigate in Lestrade's motorcar, stopping on the way at a wine merchant's establishment where Holmes purchased a small bottle of gin. He opened the bottle and sprinkled my clothing fairly liberally with the strong smelling spirit, and finally recapped the bottle and slipped it into the left inside pocket of my jacket.

The hotel's reception entrance appeared to be very much like any other establishment that rented rooms. However, as Holmes and Lestrade led me in, each holding one of my arms the whole atmosphere seemed to change. I swayed and muttered incoherently, as we had rehearsed and two burly white-coated men appeared and took over my support. The woman clerk at the desk rang a bell and a silver haired man neatly dressed in morning attire arrived. She addressed him as Dr. Richards and he cast a remonstrating eye over me. The woman asked, "Have you brought this man here for treatment, for he looks as if he has gone a little far in his addiction to require mere rest and quiet? Were you recommended to us by anyone?"

"My cousin, Charles Morton, might well require treatment. Yes, we were recommended by an ex-patient of yours." Holmes played his part to perfection as I did the best with my own role as an advanced alcoholic. The clerk asked if she could have the name of the ex-patient and Holmes responded with great inventive ability. "I did not know the lady myself, but my cousin met her and she treated him with great kindness giving him your address and her recommendation, but such was his condition that he cannot recall her name. But she gave him a photograph of herself and you may recognise her?"

As Holmes showed the photograph I fancied I noticed the woman start slightly. She showed it to Dr. Richards who displayed no emotion save for a portrayal of lack of recognition; if indeed such a lack was not genuine.

Thus far I admit that I had not realised quite how deeply involved I was, having imagined that at this point Holmes would make our excuses and we would leave for pastures old and new. Imagine then my dismay when he said to the lady clerk, "I would like to leave my cousin with you for a few days so that I can decide upon his future based on whatever advice you can give me?" He was then assured that this would be possible and the two attendants tightened their grip upon me, as it was obviously imminent that I should be frog-marched away in the care of Dr. Richards who had already taken the liberty of removing the gin bottle from my side pocket. Holmes moved over towards me and shook me by the hand, saying, "Charles, it is in your best interest. Do not worry, I will see you in a few days time." He slipped something into my breast pocket, adding, "There, you have my address so that you can write when you feel better."

As he and Lestrade made to depart it was a nightmare, or very much worse than a nightmare because it was really happening to me. I was actually going to have to stay in this haven for alcoholics, a part of the bargain I had not realised possible.

As if in a dream I waved to Holmes and Lestrade as I was led unsteadily to I knew not where!

What happened next and the horror of it all I can hardly to this day think of without a shudder. I had of course arrived in a completely sober condition but had to feign intoxication. Dr. Richards had of course no reason to suspect that I was anything but that which my appearance and rehearsed behaviour suggested. I was therefore taken into a tiled room where I was stripped and thrown into icy cold water, then towelled roughly but fortunately had my clothing returned. I was then taken to an apartment that could have passed for a somewhat Spartan hotel room, and given a foul tasting potion to drink that my sense of taste told me was a mild calming agent. Finally I was instructed to take a nap and told that I would be fetched at teatime.

Despite the sedative I had no intention of sleeping; my mind in fact was full of thoughts concerning how to make my stay at this institution as short as possible. I reviewed the situation as I knew it to be. I was here in this no doubt admirable hotel for immoderate drinkers, the object of my stay being to reduce my intake of wines, beers or spirits. I was here to try and discover if Belle Elmore had ever been an inmate, for how long and at what period. I had no idea as to the name she had used as the management, wisely, did not divulge such intimate and exclusive information. Holmes had placed what I took to be a message into my breast pocket. I removed it for the first time, only to find to my surprise the photograph of Mrs. Crippen. I sat upon my bed and studied it, not for the first time. Obviously there was only any point in my showing it to long stay or resident patients, or those who had made more than one stay any of which could have coincided with those of our quarry. Names were useless save any that I could learn by showing the picture. I pondered upon the fact that the lady may well have had hennaed red hair at the time of such a stay which could have made her appearance seem very different.

The photograph was sepia with a matt finish, which meant that had I been the owner of some red watercolour and a brush I could perhaps have made the lady in the picture more as she would have been during a possible stay at the hotel. Clearly my present status would not have quite matched a demand for watercolours and brushes. Later perhaps when I was supposed to be recovering it could have been possible without causing any suspicion, but I did not intend to stay for that long. (I had fallen in with Holmes's plan only by calming my mind with that thought).

A glance around the room revealed a wardrobe, a stand bearing a hot water jug and another bearing a washbowl. A small cupboard proved to contain cotton wool, bandages and similar items of very primitive first aid. I imagined that I might possibly use some of the cotton wool in place of the brush, and I had water in the jug, but where was I going to get the red colouration?

A search of my own clothing revealed little, save a small penknife, my hunter, and a little coinage. (Holmes had insisted on checking my pockets for anything that could have possibly aroused suspicion). I tried to think what my friend would do in this present situation. In examining the penknife I realised that although the blades were small enough for me to have been allowed to keep it, one blade had an extremely sharp point. The plan came to me quite easily; I would prick the ball of my thumb with the point of the blade, an action I knew could produce several droplets of blood.

I will not bore the reader with further details of how I managed to colour Belle's startlingly fair hair into that which could suggest the use of henna. I placed the picture in sunlight on the windowsill to dry as I tried to hide all traces of my artistic efforts. Fortunately I had managed to dry the picture before I was visited with the intention of my being 'taken down for tea'. When the gargantuan attendant eventually arrived I had the sense to arrange myself upon the bed. When he roused me I affected to be still intoxicated but to a much lesser degree than my previous histrionics had suggested. He seemed pleased with my at least partial recovery, saying, "That's better Sir, we don't want to be staggering about down in the dining rooms now do we?"

As I conversed in a purposely confused way with some of the other residents I found it hard to realise that their behaviour had been caused by real alcoholic problems and that I was the only one whose hands shook from choice! There were both men and women, most of who appeared to be reasonably respectable and coherent. Indeed I recognised a well-known actor whose name I will not betray for compassionate reasons.

"Have you just arrived?" an elderly man with grey hair and a moustache to match said to me. When I told him that I had been on the premises for a few hours he commiserated, "I know what it is like when you first arrive, it all has a feeling of unreality, but you get used to it believe me." The grey haired man examined my doctored photograph of Belle Elmore with interest, saying, "She was here the first time I was brought in. I could not believe my good fortune, asking, "When would she have been here do you think?" He looked thoughtful, then said, "Let me see, Esme Carol was already a guest here when I first arrived in March last year. I've been in and out since, you know how it is, but Esme was here attempting a permanent cure. It takes courage to do that and she was here for about three months. For much of that time she was evidently confused and sleeping for long periods, then when she started to recover she was allowed to join in activities with the rest of the guests. I left, but the next time I came in, some weeks later she was still here, and beginning to catch up on those things that had been happening during that period when she had been kept on sedatives.

Needless to say I was greatly encouraged now that I had a name that seemed to be that which Belle Elmore had used at the retreat and could hardly wait to give the information to Holmes. However, I did feel that some confirmation of what I had heard might be useful. I chatted as casually as I could and only managed to find one other of those I consorted with to have almost certainly known the lady. This was an elderly woman who was extremely shaky and perhaps not quite as reliable as my previous contact. She said, "Esme was a dear girl but kept to herself a great deal. I believe she was suffering from a very advanced state of alcoholic amnesia, seeming to have no knowledge of recent events. For example, just after the trial of that dreadful man, Crippen, she started shouting and screaming about it, to the effect that he was innocent! Well I ask you, that gives you some idea of what a dreadful state she was in." Again I could not begin to believe in my incredible good fortune and I must have been shaking with suppressed excitement because she said, "You want to get them to give you something to calm you down love." I could not resist asking, "Is that what they did with Esme?" The lady replied, "Oh yes, but they would have given her something a lot stronger than that I meant for you to ask. She didn't reappear for days, and then she hardly spoke; just kept muttering, 'It's too late …' In a right state she was."

I could have danced for joy, feeling that now it was time for me to return to Holloway and give Holmes the tidings. But I was soon to learn that this was easier said than done.

I walked purposefully to the reception area and told the clerk that important business now made it necessary for me to return to the home of my cousin in Holloway and asked for this to be arranged. But I was told that it could not and that I must be patient until my cousin called again to see me, in a day or two as had been arranged. She then said, "Furthermore

Mr. Morton your appointment with the masseur is due within fifteen minutes, so I hope you are not going to make problems!"

Looking back even though time has been the great healer I do not think I will ever forget the horror of the next half hour or so. I was taken to an apartment and given what I can only describe as a sort of Turkish bath. Then with only a towel at my waist I was subjected to the most agonising torture imaginable by a huge and horrendous woman, who threw hot and cold water on me, and then proceeded to beat me mercilessly with what seemed to be some sort of birch broom. I found later that it had been some kind of pliant twigs and that it was known as a Russian bath, and was something which would have cost me dearly in a central London hotel baths. Amazing to think that the rich will pay good money to be thus abused.

Back in my room I recovered slowly and tried to think what my next move should be, I knew that I could not survive another day in this torture chamber masquerading as a hotel for the addicted. So many wild plans passed through my mind only to be discarded as impractical. I dressed as carefully as I could in my once discarded clothes and glanced out of the window, seeking inspiration. Then it was that I saw a motorcar, and formulated my wild plan for escape. It would be possible, I decided, to climb out of the window, drop easily the eight feet to *terra firma* and to drive away in the car. I believed I could remember how Lestrade had managed the process of starting and driving his machine.

Of course I felt no guilt regarding the first part of my scheme that I managed fairly easily, making a good landing on soft grass. But the second part of the plan gave me a certain amount of trouble both with my conscience and also with its practicality. By luck, I first thought, the car appeared to be of the same popular model as the one that Lestrade owned and I tried to remember where the starting handle was stored. Eventually I found it in that portion at the rear of the vehicle that I believe is referred to as a Dickey seat. I was about to fit the handle and attend to the engine when a figure loomed up at me, grasping my arm and shouting, "Oh no you don't my lad!" To my immense relief it turned out to be Lestrade who almost at once recognised me, relaxed his grip and asked, Doctor, what DO you think you are doing?'

He explained that Holmes was at that very moment in the lobby asking to see me. We repaired to that spot, where Holmes stood, talking to the clerk. The latter turning to me and demanding to know why I was not in my room. I seem to remember muttering something all but inaudible, trying at the same time to explain to Holmes *sotto voce* that I had the information we required.

Sparing the reader from unnecessary detail it is enough to say that Holmes was able to cancel the plan for me to stay longer at the haven for unfortunates. On the way back to Holloway I regaled Lestrade and Holmes with the details of my adventure experienced in the line of duty. They both seemed to find it hard to keep straight faces, but Holmes was delighted that I had been able to get a name to fit to the photograph of Belle Elmore. He said, "You have done sterling work Watson, and your results have far exceeded my expectations regarding both the speed and the attainment. I could not have done better myself, even had I been available." I started, "What has arisen to make it impossible for you to be treated as a drunkard and beaten black and blue with twigs?" He answered softly, "Watson I understand your indignation, but I was, as Lestrade will tell you, more deeply involved with the business of the Reverend and the Major than I would wish to have been. I had a lot of explaining to do on my own behalf and yours. The bureaucrats can be tiresome my dear fellow, but I believe we now have that particular matter fully explained and accepted. Neither of the aforementioned gentlemen will be a danger to humanity for a long time to come, if indeed they avoid execution on grounds of insanity."

On our way to Hilldrop Crescent Holmes bade Lestrade stop at a newsagent's shop where he purchased three copies of *The Era*. When we were at home (if one can possibly refer to the house of such grisly memories such) he distributed these to Lestrade and myself. Opening the third copy himself he said, "If we all peruse the paper for the name that you have discovered to be our quarry we are likely to find that which we seek much more quickly."

We did not read the papers exactly, rather we scanned them for the magic words Esme Carol. It was Lestrade who first spotted our quarry. "Here we are Mr. Holmes, Doctor, she is listed in the 'Calls' as being one of the artistes appearing at the Bedford Music Hall in Camden Town. Other names mentioned are Marie Lloyd, Sam Mayo and W. C. Fields, plus full supporting programme." Holmes nodded his appreciation of Lestrade's sharp eyes. He said, "Well done Lestrade, but tell me, you know more than I do concerning popular entertainment, I imagine the fact that she is named rather than just one of the supporting company means that she is a name in the business to be reckoned with?" Lestrade said, "The fact that at least two of the others named are widely known to the public shows that they, namely Miss Lloyd and Mr. Mayo, are at the top of the bill. I know nothing of Mr. Fields, or indeed the lady that interests us, so I imagine they are mentioned as examples of the supporting company. Perhaps the other supporting acts had not been definitely fixed at the time the copy for the column went to press?"

As he had been conversing with Lestrade his fingers had continued to turn the pages and his eyes had continued in their duty as scanners. I had often admired his ability to perform two or more functions at the same time, never perhaps as much as now as he dropped the open paper on the table and said, "There is a short piece about Esme Carol here on page eight."

We each silently read the short article.

ESME CAROL OPENS IN TOWN: Esme Carol, girl of many parts, is opening in London this week after a tour of Australia. She impersonates Eva Tanguay, Ella Sheilds, Ida Barr and most remarkably the late Belle Elmore, the music hall star who was Crippen's victim and whose voice and mannerisms she has perfected.

I suppose strictly speaking Holmes finished reading the piece first, although Lestrade was the first to comment. "The fact that she impersonates Belle Elmore and uses the name that she gave to the people at the refuge would make it pretty certain that Esme Carol is really Belle Elmore. I had my doubts about Crippen's innocence, but now I am convinced that you were right all along Holmes."

It was my turn to speak but I asked a question, "Are you convinced also Holmes that Belle Elmore did not contrive the whole thing to implicate Crippen, with the dramatic results that we have seen?" But Holmes evidently did not suspect this, saying, "No Watson, according to the information you obtained at the hotel and our other discoveries, she was in a very advanced state of alcohol related illness. Belle Elmore was fighting for her life, her only desires being to regain her health and then return to the profession that she loved. She pawned the last of her quite valuable jewellery to capitalise this plan, with the help of her friend old Maude. She had no knowledge of the flesh under the basement floor and had no reason to believe that anyone would believe that she had been murdered. Crippen knew that there had been bad blood between Belle and his own son and believed that her disappearance meant that his son had murdered her. Hoping to give the young man a chance to get away he made the decoy play of dressing Miss le Neve as his son with the results that we know. The son in his turn believed that Belle's disappearance meant that his father had murdered her. The fact that both of them continued in these beliefs is borne out by their shared desire not to implicate each other at Crippen's trial. Belle of course knew nothing of any of this until it was far too late to make an intervention. Then on reflection she decided, with Miss le Neve so lightly dealt with, to leave well alone and try and get on with her life."

Everything seemed to fit the events, which had been so much complicated by the activities of the two bizarre characters, one of which had occupied Crippen's house before him. I supposed all that remained was to make absolutely sure of our facts by going to the Bedford Music Hall in Camden Town.

When I bought three stalls for the first house I managed to find out the approximate time of Miss Esme Carol's appearance. I was told that she would appear immediately before the interval, at about six-forty. Although I have enjoyed a variety entertainment from time to time, ever since my student days I knew from experience that Holmes was not a lover of any form of light entertainment. From kindness I therefore suggested that we station ourselves in the stalls bar and take up our seats just before Esme Carols number went up on the indicator. As we sat there, Lestrade with his glass of ale, Holmes with his brandy and water and I with my sherry, we could hear the artistes, the applause and occasional laughter: indeed we could actually see the stage reflected on one of the glass doors of the bar. We heard the strains of a Strauss waltz as the reflection showed me two gymnasts lifting each other and performing a terrifying head to head balance, yet I knew that their lifetime of dedication and practice would have failed to interest my friend. The performing dogs that followed jumping tiny fences caused Sherlock Holmes to turn his back upon the reflection. The sad eyed comedian in his blazer and straw hat found Holmes with his head deep in his hands, lest he should chance to hear that which he did not see.

Then when I consulted my hunter and announced that it was time to take our seats it was a very different Sherlock Holmes that accompanied us. As the band in the pit played a lively air we watched the entrance of Esme Carol who we now knew almost beyond doubt to be the late Belle Elmore. Of course we knew her appearance from photographs, and could immediately see a striking likeness, despite the hennaed hair. She wore a simple black dress with sequins across the neckline and carried a large dress handbag from which she took a scarf here and a fan there to present enhancement to her impersonations. She sang I Don't Care and the audience showed their approval and I could tell that the impersonation of the famous Eva Tanguay was a good one.

(Despite never having seen or heard the famous American chanteuse myself).

With some courage she impersonated the great Marie Lloyd herself who would later in the programme appear as its star. But when she gave her impersonation of Belle Elmore that effect was electric. Obviously Belle had been more popular with audiences than some had led us to believe. I remarked as much to Holmes very quietly, behind my programme. He equally quietly replied, "Did not Clarkson Rose suggest as much? Journalists will always find some unpleasantness concerning popular personalities if it suits their purpose, especially when they are believed as Miss Elmore was, to be deceased."

After the interval we made our way from the theatre and Holmes remarked to me, "I suppose really we have to obtain our final proof, from Miss Carol." He headed towards the notice that indicated 'To The Stage Door'. Then suddenly he made a signal to us to stop and we saw why he had ceased to move. There, just disappearing into the alley leading to the stage door was old Maude, with her trolley. Holmes smiled broadly as he said to us, "There I think goes our final proof. I do not believe we need trouble Miss Carol!" Lestrade and I grasped his meaning at once.

Epilogue

At Simpson's

Later that same evening when Lestrade had made his excuses to depart, Holmes and I took a farewell meal at Simpson's in the Strand. On the morrow I knew my friend would depart for the Sussex coast, his vacation from bee-keeping over. I knew that his feelings were mixed. There was a part of him that wanted to stay and continue investigations like those of the past few days, during which we had proved, at least to ourselves that the most famous murderer of them all was innocent, and narrowly missed being made into pork pies. As for my own feelings, I had enjoyed the thrills of the chase, for the game had well and truly been afoot; yet cannot pretend to the reader that I had enjoyed playing the part of an alcoholic. We said little, we were just two old friends enjoying each others' company. Holmes had already explained everything to my understanding, if not satisfaction. But then suddenly one loose end seemed to worry my mind that had already accepted so much that had seemed improbable.

I asked, "Holmes, there is just one thing that still needs a little clarification. Why did those two evil men hide those bones in the attic in such a vulnerable place rather than disposing of them as they had others?"

Sherlock Holmes grinned wickedly as he said, "My dear fellow, it was I who hid the bones for you to find. I bought a couple of skeletons from the shop in Praed Street, where the medical students buy them. I doctored them and mixed them up. Iodine and a sharp knife can work wonders! That is why I told you that you need not start your night vigil at the Crippen house until the second evening, since I needed the intervening time to gather and plant them there for you to find."

I understood on reflection what he had done but still did not understand. I asked, "But Holmes … why?"

My friend chuckled a little and then replied, "If you cast your mind back Watson to that particular time in our recent adventures you will remember that you were on the brink of telling me that you could spare no more time to what you secretly considered to be a lost cause. I had to do something to stimulate your interest, and it worked, did it not?"

Sherlock Holmes will return
in a new adventure

**Sherlock Holmes
and the
Frightened Chambermaid**

by

John Hall

"With five volumes you could fill that gap on that second shelf"
(Sherlock Holmes, *The Empty House*)

So why not collect all 43 murder mysteries from Baker Street Studios? Available from all good bookshops, or direct from the publisher with free U.K. postage & packing at just £7.50 each. Alternatively you can get full details of all our publications, including our range of audio books, and order on-line where you can also join our mailing list and see our latest special offers.

THE ADVENTURE OF THE SPANISH DRUMS
THE CASE OF THE MISSING STRADIVARIUS*
THE ELEMENTARY CASES OF SHERLOCK HOLMES
IN THE DEAD OF WINTER**
MYSTERY OF A HANSOM CAB
SHERLOCK HOLMES: A DUEL WITH THE DEVIL
SHERLOCK HOLMES AND THE ABBEY SCHOOL MYSTERY
SHERLOCK HOLMES AND THE ADLER PAPERS
SHERLOCK HOLMES AND THE BAKER STREET DOZEN
SHERLOCK HOLMES AND THE BOULEVARD ASSASSIN
SHERLOCK HOLMES AND THE CHILFORD RIPPER
SHERLOCK HOLMES AND THE CHINESE JUNK AFFAIR
SHERLOCK HOLMES AND THE CIRCUS OF FEAR
SHERLOCK HOLMES AND THE DISAPPEARING PRINCE
SHERLOCK HOLMES AND THE DISGRACED INSPECTOR
SHERLOCK HOLMES AND THE EGYPTIAN HALL ADVENTURE
SHERLOCK HOLMES AND THE FRIGHTENED GOLFER
SHERLOCK HOLMES AND THE GIANT'S HAND
SHERLOCK HOLMES AND THE GREYFRIARS SCHOOL MYSTERY
SHERLOCK HOLMES AND THE HAMMERFORD WILL
SHERLOCK HOLMES AND THE HOLBORN EMPORIUM
SHERLOCK HOLMES AND THE HOUDINI BIRTHRIGHT
SHERLOCK HOLMES AND THE LONGACRE VAMPIRE
SHERLOCK HOLMES AND THE MAN WHO LOST HIMSELF
SHERLOCK HOLMES AND THE MORPHINE GAMBIT
SHERLOCK HOLMES AND THE SANDRINGHAM HOUSE MYSTERY
SHERLOCK HOLMES AND THE SECRET MISSION
SHERLOCK HOLMES AND THE SECRET SEVEN
SHERLOCK HOLMES AND THE TANDRIDGE HALL MYSTERY
SHERLOCK HOLMES AND THE TELEPHONE MURDER MYSTERY
SHERLOCK HOLMES AND THE THEATRE OF DEATH
SHERLOCK HOLMES AND THE THREE POISONED PAWNS
SHERLOCK HOLMES AND THE TITANTIC TRAGEDY
SHERLOCK HOLMES AND THE TOMB OF TERROR
SHERLOCK HOLMES AND THE YULE-TIDE MYSTERY
SHERLOCK HOLMES AT THE RAFFLES HOTEL
SHERLOCK HOLMES AT THE VARIETIES
SHERLOCK HOLMES ON THE WESTERN FRONT
SHERLOCK HOLMES: THE GHOST OF BAKER STREET
SPECIAL COMMISSION
THE TORMENT OF SHERLOCK HOLMES
THE TRAVELS OF SHERLOCK HOLMES
WATSON'S LAST CASE

* £15.99 HARDBACK ONLY   ** £8.50

Baker Street Studios Limited, Endeavour House, 170 Woodland Road, Sawston, Cambridge CB22 3DX
www.breesebooks.com, sales@breesebooks.com

3